Prais...

I don't have a lot o...
I couldn't wait to get back to this book...
that good.
—Sarah N

Anyone with self-esteem issues should read every word in this riveting and uplifting story.
—Heidi W

This is a "can't put it down" book. From the beginning to end, I was mesmerized by the story of the author's life. Her inner calling to take on the trauma of a childhood filled with pain and turn it into something beautiful is inspiring.
—Gena W

I picked up your book this morning. I figured I'd get a start on it before starting everything else I had to do today, and perhaps dig into it more this weekend. So here I sit unshowered, teeth unbrushed, still in my nightie at 3pm, and I finished this book!!! It was awesome. LOVED it.
—Piper C

You must read this book. It speaks directly to your heart. This beautifully written book has meaning for anyone that is scarred, physically, emotionally or mentally. Lesia shares her story with bravery and humility.
—Marge C

I picked up *Heart of Fire* this morning and could not stop reading until I finished. In one day!! I didn't want it to end! I've never read such love, caring and courage Lesia shared!!!! I cried and laughed throughout reading this book!
—Carol Ann

What an amazing story. The journey this book takes you on is heartwarming. It is so well written that as sad as it was at times she was able to lift you up as fast. I enjoyed every page.
—Kathleen C

I had started reading another book I was very interested in and a new friend gave me this book to read. I started on page one and I couldn't put the book down. I was no longer interested in the other book and finished *Heart of Fire* in no time at all. It was captivating!

—Amazon review

Such courage and strength. Once I picked up the book I couldn't put it down. I recommend it to everyone. —Amazon review

Loved this book. I read it in one day. I could not put it down. The story is amazing and inspirational. — Amazon review

Heart of Fire is an amazing book that will captivate you from the very first page and keep you turning the pages until the conclusion. I
enjoyed it so much that I read it in one sitting, then months later took it on an airline flight to enjoy again. —Annie R

It's been a long time since I've read a book in one day, but I seriously could not put this one down! This story will reach in and grab a part of you that is both tender and traumatic. Be prepared to laugh and cry over and over. —Julie S

A really inspirational book! A great story of personal triumph over heartbreaking adversity. Her story is about more than her own survival but about helping others navigate the same hard road. A great read from start to finish! —Jeffery Exum

An incredible story of triumph over tragedy. This book is a totally gripping, vulnerable account of a little girl who has blossomed into an extraordinary woman in every way. —Antoinette W

Tumble
Weed

Lesia Stockall Cartelli
author of the award-winning *Heart of Fire*

Tumble Weed

Discovering Gifts from Trauma

Tumbleweed
Discovering Gifts from Trauma
© 2024 Lesia Stockall Cartelli

All rights reserved.

This book or any portion thereof may not be reproduced or used in any manner whatsoever without the written permission of the publisher except for the use of brief quotations in a book review.

Cover and Interior Design:
Rebecca Finkel, F + P Graphic Design, FPGD.com

Books may be purchased in quantity
through the author's website: LesiaCartelli.com

Library of Congress Control Number: data on file
ISBN paperback: 978-0-9904307-4-2
ISBN eBook: 978-0-9904307-5-9

Inspiration | Trauma | Mental Health | Success

First Edition
Printed in the USA

*To Bently,
my furry heart.*

Contents

First Thoughts xi

1 Clarence 1

2 Explosion Echo 15

3 "Katie, Breathe" 37

4 Heart Work 49

5 Two Days in December 67

6 Dream Maker 81

7 "He*art* in Heaven" 107

8 "I Got You" 119

9 Tumbleweed 135

Final Thoughts 155

Lesia Stockall Cartelli 159

First Thoughts

There is always more to the story. This is the more, *Tumbleweed*. It's been ten years since I wrote my first book, *Heart of Fire*. I had no intention of writing a second book, but the lessons, magical moments, and levels of awareness of how our life unfolds based on our thoughts and expands to what we desire, all deserves to be told.

Paying attention to what goes on around us, daily, is exhausting but can be entertaining and is key to personal growth. It also brings clarity and peace if you look with courage and not with fear.

In writing this book, I'm deeply grateful for the side conversations with people I trust. Dr. LeighAnn Price made herself available day or night answering my questions on how much to reveal in tender stories, or omit, or simply share. Dr. Price became my true north in this endeavor. Without her endless encouragement I'd still be sitting with an outline wondering if it was time to go for a walk, instead. To my beautiful friend Karen who picked me up for what was to be an evening of fine dining, that suddenly turned into my uncontrollable sobs at the linen dressed table before the wine was even served. "So how is your book coming along" was all she needed to ask. It was the day I completed the chapters about my grandpa and the pieces I never knew. The waiter was terrified of my tears and the service rapidly declined. Karen scooped her arm up under mine and led me to the car to sit with me while I sobbed in private. Once I was able to catch my breath, she drove to a roadside café where we ate burgers and fries—landing at a more suitable place for raw emotions.

I'm grateful for my mother and siblings who were willing to answer painful hard questions of the past. To the many people in this book who allowed me to share our experiences together, your names may have been changed but your spirits are here. To Bently, my amazing brown standard poodle, who seemed to know what I was writing before I did. And to my husband who continues to work keeping the circus in town.

I'm not sure where I get the courage to share the stories in this book that need to be told. I'm often asked, "Is it cathartic to reveal your life lessons?" I struggle with the word "cathartic." Some of what is written in this book was difficult to write. Other parts brought up memories of laughter and comfort. I hope both touch your heart.

—Lesia

1
Clarence

Trusting our path chases away the uncertainty, sleepless nights, and overall anxiety we bring upon ourselves. Believing that our challenges are for a good reason delivers a calm feeling that all will be okay.

If an angel had sat me down before my birth and told me what my life would entail, it would have seemed impossible to endure those challenges and still find a big love for living. "May I pick a different life from your bag of life choices, please?"

I was raised in a large, chaotic family by an untreated bipolar, alcoholic father and a mother who desperately tried to hold us together. We moved nearly every year. I endured severe burns over half of my body in a natural gas explosion at my grandparents' home. Not a spoon or fork survived; everything was reduced to ash. Painful losses of family and friends, including finding my grandmother dead when I was fifteen, became my normal. If given the choice, I would have passed on this life.

But now, when I gaze behind me, I see the love that came from rejection, the trust born from betrayal, laughter that sadness taught me, gratitude that stemmed from loss, self-respect that rose from self-doubt, and the faith that came from forsakenness. This life is worth the pain, especially when I can turn up the light inside to dissolve the darkness.

I often think about the movie classic *It's a Wonderful Life*, starring Jimmy Stewart as George Bailey and Henry Travers as his angel, Clarence. The message is simple: we are right where we belong. Although I've thought life would be better if I moved to a different city or changed careers or life partners, it's important that I trust my path. We can grow strong right where we stand and create the life we desire. Even painful traumatic events such as divorce, the loss of a job, injury, betrayal, illness, or death can be transformed into something beautiful. Yes, I, too, grieve over the losses, but ultimately, we can heal.

> *Don't waste the hurt. Feeling hurt is the greatest teacher. Sit with the uncomfortable feelings, embrace them, honor them, then let them go.*

Trusting my path has been hard, especially when it's covered in dirt, washed out with potholes, or winding to a dead end. When I raise my head, I see flowers that grow along the path's edge. I'm encouraged to look around, see the beauty, and stay open to opportunities, even when a situation appears hopeless. It may take time, but things always work out for our highest good.

Like George Bailey in that Christmas classic, I didn't meet my angels until my darkest hour. At just nine years old, I lay burning alive from a gas explosion at my grandparents' home. Trapped in the basement of an inferno. I pulled myself over the scorching rubble to reach the light shining through a hole to the outside. The light served two purposes: one, to show me an exit; the other, to force me to look up. As I crawled over searing mounds of debris, inching my way out of this hell, three angels appeared in the light between me and the hole—one in front, two behind. They stood elevated in this bright white light, so bright it was almost blue. I struggled to keep my eyes open to see the light beams that pierced through the smoke and flames. As soon as I saw the angels, my pain began to subside, but my urgency to escape remained.

I stretched for them, expecting to be lifted into their arms for safety. They didn't extend a welcome but rather communicated an understanding that I was to get through this horrific event—and this life—and they would take care of me. In exchange for their protection, I needed to trust what was coming and extend my heart to others. In that moment,

I would've agreed to anything if it meant getting out of this flaming debris. The angels' presence calmed every cell in my being. I could finally take a breath without the burn sensation in my lungs ... a breath I needed to escape.

The same three angels appeared to me a second time a few nights later as I lay under the stiff, scratchy hospital sheets, heavily medicated. When I first saw them, I thought they were there to finally retrieve me. I felt myself rise above the bed, wanting to get closer, closer than in the basement. But their message was the same: trust your path, and we will never leave you. My pain left again. Love took over, a pure, unconditional love.

Ever since I met my angels, I knew I couldn't waste my pain. I had to transform it into something positive that brought light and healing to the world. It took me years to accept that this horrendous accident was merely preparing me for my life's work. I have not seen the angels again as clearly as when they first appeared to me in their initial form, but I have felt their presence often.

It's a Wonderful Life was also my father's favorite movie. He felt he didn't fit in, but rarely played the victim. My father never had a normal job that I can remember. He constantly bought, sold, and traded boats, motorcycles, cars, art, and houses. He made a lot of money and spent even more. He told me once that if he died with five dollars in his pocket, "I miscalculated."

He taught me about the fragility of life (surviving an explosion cemented that message), and it was up to me to find or create joy in the simplest moments. His creativity was constantly in overdrive. Often, while enjoying a meal out, he'd pick up his napkin and fold it into a funny shape, then would encourage the table, and often the entire restaurant to play along. We were never far from the circus when we were with him. He *was* the circus.

But he could be devastatingly harsh, too. While I was in the hospital after my accident, I went through a low period, not complying with my nurses and doctors and treating my mom poorly. I knew I was sinking into darkness. My father arrived, sent my mother home, and gave me a big, loud, scary lecture about how this accident was tearing the family up. I suspected things were bad at home, worse than before the explosion. I could hear whispers in the hall from my visitors how my one sibling didn't come home, another refused to go to school, and my now homeless grandparents were living in our house amidst the well-established chaos.

> It helps to recognize that the people closest to us may be at war with themselves. It's our duty to protect ourselves and not become collateral damage from their war.

"Lesia, we lost everything!" My father stomped around the tiny room like a caged animal as my eyes, half covered in crusty bandages, followed his movements. "My mother and father, your grandparents, who have worked hard and saved every penny to prepare for their future, now have nothing and are sleeping on our couches. You are not alone in your pity!" He said if I continued to feel sorry for myself, I might as well not have survived the explosion because the family didn't need any more victims. "Until you decide what path you're going to take, no one will be coming to visit you."

After he left, I lay stunned, wondering what had happened at home that day to push him over the edge. How did he think I could handle what he had to say? What I needed to hear from him was that our telephone at home was ringing off the hook day and night from people who cared about us and wanted to help. I needed to hear how my mom had to place a notebook next to the telephone so we could keep a running list of callers. I needed to hear that my friends from school cared; my teachers, neighbors, and relatives reached out to offer help. I needed to know that bags of get-well cards and letters from my school arrived on our doorstep. I needed to hear that the East Detroit Fire Department knocked on our door with eight hundred dollars to give my grandpa. I needed to hear that everyone was pulling for me, loved me, and cared about our family. I needed to hear all this that day, not decades later.

I didn't know it then, but my father's father had also survived a catastrophic explosion, losing everything as a boy of thirteen. Two big chemical explosions, one lifetime. Trauma can hijack the soul, and it can be passed from one generation to the next. My trauma was both inherited and experienced. Fifty-two years after an explosion took his childhood home, my grandfather sat in an ambulance with me, my skin still burning from the explosion at his house, the family trauma repeating itself. I just didn't know it at the time. Family secrets gnaw away at the spirit.

I've yearned for, witnessed, and experienced so many levels of healing from trauma: physical, financial, emotional, sexual, and spiritual. In healthcare, initially saving a patient's life is number one: critical care, surgeries, ongoing reconstruction, physical therapy, learning how to walk, talk, swallow, and function with everyday life.

The true hard work of survival comes barreling down the path when trauma patients leave the protective womb of the hospital. I was scared to leave Children's Hospital in Detroit, where I spent months being treated. During my daily bandage changes I learned which nurse was rough and which was gentle. I knew no one at home had this skill. I also loved the schedule of three meals a day, no one shouting, and no phone calls from collection agencies. As traumatizing as the hospital treatments were—the worst was the debriding of dead skin in the tub rooms—the prospect of stares, questions, and rejection once I left the hospital trumped the tub experience.

Trauma can transform the strongest sense of self into self-hatred, addiction, and isolation. Those who have endured a severe traumatic event may also experience the loss of family (due to dynamics around the event), friends, and ultimately the self as they knew it. After watching and experiencing the long-term effects of trauma, I had to do something for myself and those around me to create a fulfilling life.

For the past thirty years, I have built multidisciplinary teams of mental and physical healthcare professionals and launched, designed, and directed psychosocial programs for people who have been through severe traumas. Twenty years ago, I created Angel Faces, a 501(c)(3) nonprofit organization. We run retreats for adolescent girls and young women after they are discharged from the hospital wounded, scared, and marked with scars.

Transforming trauma into something positive brings boundless rewards.

I take them to a private resort-like setting where, with my team and devoted volunteers, the girls and women have a safe space to talk about (and ultimately embrace) the avoidant details of their accident. They begin to understand the gifts from their tragic experience, look at the possibility of forgiveness, and discover self-acceptance. When we have the courage to look at our circumstances, we can identify and transform the gifts from trauma. There are times during the week when our laughter is used to cradle the pain, particularly amongst the volunteers. These fits of laughter help us sleep at night, otherwise our tears would soak the bed.

I've had the privilege of seeing deep into the heart of wounded souls. It's messy, dark, and raw inside. At each retreat, as I stand to deliver my welcome at orientation, I see pieces of my own heart staring back at me. I think of Clarence and know I'm right where I belong.

I see that people who survive traumatic events find one another's wounds, as though a magnetic thread weaves through them connecting their agony. At Angel Faces, I watch those threads come together and weave a blanket of comfort, hope, and friendships to create a better life.

Over the years running the retreats, I've also witnessed numerous acts of courage and life-changing breakthroughs. Bounlod, whose arms were medically severed above the elbow from burns in a house fire in Laos, sat and watched other girls suit up to scale a climbing wall. I asked her, "Bounlod, do you want to do this?"

"Ms. Lesia, I can't. Look at me. I have no arms."

I silently agreed. But my courage pushed me to approach our master climbing instructor, who had been watching Bounlod.

"Jonathon, can your team find a way?" I whispered. "Can she climb?" With watery sparkles in both our eyes, he summoned his crew, altered his equipment, and began to strap a harness on Bounlod.

While this was going on, I saw Campbell sitting on the bench, observing. Campbell, age nineteen, had lost all tendons and muscles in both her legs in a house fire in Texas. She can walk only with assistive devices and quite gingerly at best. I smiled at Campbell and mouthed, "You want to try?"

She bit her bottom lip, clasped her hands together, and nodded. Within thirty minutes, Bounlod and Campbell began to scale the wall together, sharing a ferocious heart of determination as deafening cheers rose up from below. Bravery is infectious. Resilience emerges at the hint of another's courage.

Courage also comes from within. Jody wrote a lengthy letter forgiving her mother for allowing her boyfriend to cook meth in the garage, leading to the explosion that severely burned Jody at age four. Numerous girls trusted us enough to reveal they were being abused at home. They knew we had to report this to Child Protective Services, and they may be taken away from their family, but they acted courageously.

The girls who come to the retreat to heal and strive for a better life are helping not only themselves. Whether they understand it yet or not, they are also taking steps to stop the generational transfer of trauma. I have been recognized for my work by CNN, 20/20, People magazine, Associated Press, Dr. Phil, and numerous organizations, but the true reward is when one of my girls transforms her trauma into action that helps herself and others.

Trauma ripples outward, like the pebble tossed into the pond. I once shared a drawing from one of our girls with her surgeon. The assignment was for our girls to draw a picture of how they saw their life. As we sat at lunch, he looked at the drawing for a long time, tears filling his eyes. He said with a quivering voice, "Lesia, our patients are not the only ones that feel their pain." I've learned the best surgeons are the ones who are not afraid to feel their heart.

When I drive with my husband in a career firefighter in San Diego, he will point out a tree, cliff, or curve in the road where he'll retell, in grave detail, who died at that scene and how. The visions of witnessing or hearing of a traumatic event stick to us like superglue. I attended a conference on critical incident stress management in Arizona and was surprised to learn of an overlooked profession that is greatly impacted by trauma: train conductors nd engineers. When someone chooses to end their life by jumping in front of a moving train, the conductor or engineer involved wrestles with intense guilt and often retires early.

Little by little, we are becoming better at understanding the ripple effects of trauma and the real work of healing. With post-traumatic stress disorder and suicides on the rise among first responders, including doctors, many police and fire departments, military branches and hospitals are finally organizing peer support groups to manage these silent creepers.

Staying open to my life's path, while looking for the good and the meaning around me, has helped me heal. As you turn these pages, look at the events in your own life—the traumatic, trivial, unfortunate, or unbecoming—and consider their hidden gifts.

You'll read how I learned the power of never giving up from a family that I first dismissed as a hot mess while judging their poor packing choices in the security line at the airport. In my darkest hours as the CEO of Angel Faces, I was saved by the hope and energy I put into the world years earlier. Traveling to Nova Scotia, Canada, to uncover my own family's generational trauma and better understand my grandfather's behavior on that fateful day of the explosion gave me more compassion than I could explain, even years after Grandpa's death.

It's a wonderful life, if we decide it is.

After I collided with a tumbleweed doing ninety miles per hour on my motorcycle, I began to see clearly what happens when emotional pain is avoided and goes untreated. We stuff our emotional wounds deep into our gut to avoid their debilitating wrath. Eventually they will tackle us, even when we do all we can to avoid facing the truth.

You'll see that difficult challenges have impacted virtually every facet of my life to teach me lessons or offer opportunities for peace. My journey has taught me that helping others is the purest way to transform pain. It brings heartache but also profound blessings. When I finally learned to trust my life's path, sometimes with a little help from my angels, I found meaning and discovered the magnetic thread that connects us all, injured or not.

Bounlod finds courage to climb

2
Explosion Echo

*Pain is pain, love is love, and the depth of either
is not to be measured, compared, or judged
but acknowledged and embraced.*

One snowy afternoon in 1969, my childhood ended abruptly. I woke up in my toasty bed and tiptoed across the creaky wooden floor to not wake my sister. But when I sprung open the shutters to discover a thick blanket of snow, I squealed, "Look, it snowed!" I ran to my siblings' rooms to announce, "It snowed—and a lot!" This was going to be an exceptional day. I could feel it. Careful not to trip on dog toys or a basket of unfolded laundry, I ran down the stairs in my worn flannel pajamas and torn socks to unlatch the front door and see how deep the snow was.

Nine years old and the youngest of five children, I had to work hard to be included. My siblings were always trying to ditch me, but I usually caught up to them. The alternative was to cry to Mom that no one wanted to play with me. The first choice was more fun. I was willing to play any game, or at least try, if they would just let me.

My loud and giddy response to snow had woken up the entire family except Dad, who always slept in after late nights at the Poison Apple, our nightclub. I poured a bowl of stale cereal I found in the back of the cupboard, checked the date on the milk carton, then chomped on the kernels while envisioning sliding down the hill in our yard on garbage can lids. Playtime in the snow flew by, and before long it was time to head to my grandparents' home for our traditional Sunday dinner. It was the only tradition I knew. My grandparents—my dad's parents—lived a steady lifestyle, and their orderly home was the only stable environment we knew. Going there for Sunday dinners was a guarantee of being served pure, gentle love and hot, home-cooked southern food with a delicious dessert, with no drinking, fighting, swearing, or feeling left out.

My grandparents owned a small one-story home with two bedrooms, one bathroom, and a finished basement with a pool table. Our home was much bigger, but ours was full of daily chaos, problems, and uncertainty stemming from my father's grandiose idealism mixed with alcohol, too little money, or too much. Usually, we all went to Sunday dinner at my grandparents' together, but this Sunday my siblings seemed to have other plans, and my mother was dealing with my father's hangover, again.

Mom looked at my oldest sister, Chris. "Why don't you and Gordy [her boyfriend] take Lesia and head on over to Bea and Burt's for dinner. We'll be there soon, as soon as I can get your father up." Her sigh when she referenced my father was heavy and familiar.

The three of us knocked, then pushed through my grandparents' front door to escape the cold. The tiny living room was filled with six of my family members. I didn't know my uncle and cousins were coming for dinner, too. I was excited because we rarely saw them. My cousin Kimmy was a few years younger, so I could boss her around, but we liked playing together.

> *A traumatic event teaches us to become aware of our vulnerabilities and uncovers our resilience.*

No matter how tiny her kitchen or her house, Grandma always invited all family to Sunday dinner for a delicious meal, enough for an army and leftovers. That was my grandmother's gift; she was a domestic goddess. She would start cooking and baking on Wednesday for Sunday's dinner. We ate at portable card tables, her sewing machine cabinet, or a makeshift cardboard box. Everyone was welcome.

As soon as we stepped inside, a wave of noxious odor mixed with a roast overcame us. I wanted to puke up the stale cereal I had for breakfast. I overheard my sister tell my grandmother the house smelled of gas. My grandmother explained, while opening windows, that she had been smelling gas for a few days. The gas company came and inspected the house yesterday, she said. They acknowledged the odor and said they would return on Monday when their offices were open.

Grandma sent me and Kimmy to the basement to play while dinner was being prepared. The odor seemed worse down there, but I wasn't going to complain as we were rarely allowed in the basement without an adult, so this felt special. As I leaned against a metal pipe by the furnace, covering my eyes and counting down for our first game of hide-and-seek, the whole house exploded. The point of ignition, the pilot light on the furnace, three feet from where I stood.

Catholic nuns are clothed in compassion, yet they are the founders of tough love.

My seven family members upstairs were thrown out of the house, while Gordy, a hefty football player, fell through the collapsed floor into the basement. He was able to reach Kimmy from the sound of her screams while I crawled to the intense white light coming from a hole at the top of the broken staircase. I encountered my angels for the first time. I climbed over the rubble to squeeze through the hole to the snow-covered yard.

A month prior, in fourth grade at St. Ambrose, a nun stood at the front of class, shook her boney finger at us, and told us if we ever caught on fire to roll in dirt. That stayed with me. The only dirt I knew was in my grandpa's garden behind his garage. Surely it was frozen over, but I didn't care. The snow would help extinguish my burning flesh. While lying in the garden, I faintly heard my name. As I stumbled toward the sirens and flashing lights, my sister found me and pulled me over a massive pile of bricks, what was once their chimney. We gathered at the house next door for shelter until the ambulances arrived.

In the chaos following the explosion, people ran everywhere, shouting and screaming. Neighbors dashed to the scene, their tears flowing like rivers. The police arrived and began to take control of the growing crowds on the sidewalk.

As I was carried to the ambulance and placed on a gurney, I lifted my head to see the last standing wall of the home collapse onto the enormous inferno. The horror was too much; I quickly looked away. My skin continued to sear from the burns. I caught my reflection in the ambulance window. My hair looked like a black Brillo pad, the kind my mother used to scrub pans. My golden locks were gone. My face began to rapidly swell, making slits for my eyes to peek through. I hardly recognized myself.

I heard my grandfather's voice. Two large firemen, one under each arm, were muscling him toward the ambulance. Grandpa seemed confused and was combative. He kept repeating, "I'm looking for my family. Where's my mother? I need to get them out!" The firemen kept reassuring him that everyone was out of the fire. Grandpa refused to believe them. "No, let go of me!" His voice wailed in agony as he attempted to wrench free. "I can hear them screaming! They are trapped in the house!"

One firefighter turned to the captain and reported that all victims in the house were accounted for. The captain, his face covered in ash, placed his massive, gloved hands on Grandpa's shoulders. "Sir, who else is in the house?" My grandfather continued to beg for help to get his family out. The captain shouted above the roar of the flames to the fire crews, "Do an immediate secondary search! Now!"

Finally, my voice, pinched from inhaling so much smoke, squeaked out. "Grandpa, I'm right here; we are all safe!" I had no idea if that was true; I was trusting what I overheard the firefighters say. In truth, I thought he just didn't recognize me because I was so badly burned. I wanted to sleep. I wanted all this to end. I couldn't handle seeing my grandfather, always clean, strong, and stoic, now seeming weak, his clothes dirty and torn, his face bloodied and covered in shards of glass and ash. His mother and family? I had never heard him speak of a family other than us. My parents and siblings—we were his only family.

The pain took over. My eyes swelled shut, and the world went dark.

My grandfather was born in 1904 in Halifax, Nova Scotia. The fourth of eleven children, his father, my great-grandfather, was a conductor with the Canadian Pacific Railway while his mother stayed home to care for their brood. On the morning of December 6, 1917, the height of World War I, when my grandpa was thirteen, there was a massive explosion in Halifax Harbor. A French cargo ship, *SS Mont-Blanc*, filled to the deck with TNT and benzol, collided with the Norwegian vessel *SS Imo*. The blast was the largest man-made explosion at the time, releasing the energy of about 2.9 kilotons of TNT. Two thousand two hundred and forty people were incinerated, and nine thousand were seriously injured and blinded by flying glass and debris.

> Family secrets can bond the bloodline but can choke out the joy at family gatherings. To some members in the family, the elephant in the center of the room is hot pink; to others, it's camouflaged. It's a personal choice.

Halifax, the last harbor before crossing the Atlantic Ocean to Europe, was an area targeted by Germans during the war. To prevent an attack, steel nets were placed at the entrance to prevent German submarines from entering the harbor. The nets were raised at dusk and dropped at dawn. The *Mont-Blanc* arrived late at Halifax Harbor and was forced to anchor outside the underwater net all night with volatile cargo, an easy target for attack. The *Imo*, on its way to depart the harbor, got stuck on the other side of the net and now had to wait for morning.

As the nets were lowered at daybreak, both ships pushed forward. When they collided, the impact damaged the benzol barrels stored on the deck of the *Mont-Blanc*, leaking vapors ignited by sparks from the collision, setting off a fire on board that quickly grew out of control. When the fire started, people in the harbor district ran to the water's edge to watch. The fire brigade and other rescue workers rushed to the scene. As word spread of a fire, hundreds of people in the town, including my family, ran to their windows to watch

The TNT on the *Mont-Blanc* ignited, and the ship exploded into tiny pieces. A massive, 9,000-degree fireball shot across the water at 3,300 feet per second. White-hot shards of iron from both ships rained down upon Halifax. A half-ton piece of the *Mont-Blanc's* anchor landed two miles south of Halifax Harbor. An area of more than four hundred acres was reduced to dust by the explosion. The harbor floor was momentarily exposed by the volume of water displaced. Immediately, a tsunami formed to fill the hole. The *Imo* was carried onto the shore at Dartmouth, across the harbor.

With scorching fire, toxic smoke, raining explosives, and flooding, every building within two miles was destroyed. People on the shore were turned to dust. The hundreds who had been watching the fire from their homes, like my family, were blinded when the blast shattered their windows. Overturned stoves and lamps started fires in houses throughout Halifax and beyond. Many families, mine included, would never be the same. I lost fourteen family members that day.

My grandpa and his younger siblings were climbing the steps to their school when the explosion occurred. It blew them off the stairs onto their backs in the gravel. They dusted themselves off and ran home, passing many homes ablaze with people running and screaming in the chaos. They passed neighbors who were either frozen in shock, injured beyond capacity, or dead. In the madness, a man recognized my grandpa and his younger siblings. He quickly gathered them together and turned them around to prevent them from seeing the horrors of their street and home.

He led them on foot over a steep hill to a town called Bedford, ten miles away from the terrible inferno. With every step, they cried and whimpered, asking for their mother and other siblings. In Bedford lived friends of our family who had a large farm. It was the only place this man knew to take them. My grandpa and his siblings stayed at the farm for three days, where they were fed and cared for. Nourishment for their bodies, but nothing for their souls. With each hour, more news of the explosion and the enormous number of casualties reached the farm.

My great-grandfather was working on the railway when he heard the massive explosion. He raced through the streets of burning houses to find his own home ablaze, arriving just after my grandpa and siblings had been whisked away. He attempted to rescue his wife and children, but it was too late. He sat and wept by the house for hours until he was able to battle the heat and embers and carry out the bodies of his wife, daughter, and first grandbaby.

Two other sons and another daughter were also in the house and miraculously survived. Russell, nineteen, was asleep on the third floor after working the graveyard shift at the railway. The blast blew him across the street onto the roof of a small orphanage. The other son, Teddy, age five, was sitting on the lap of my grandpa's sister, Grace, watching the fire in the harbor. Teddy was blinded by shattered glass, his face left scarred. Grace was not hurt.

My great-grandpa searched endlessly for the rest of his children. Hundreds of others combed through piles of embers to find their missing families, asking anyone if they had seen them and constantly checking lists posted to what was left of any random building. My great-grandpa feared his children, too, had perished in the explosion.

Two days prior to the explosion, my great-grandparents' daughter-in-law, Gertie, had arrived by train from Bedford to share the joyous news that she was pregnant. The Canadian military, in their search and recovery efforts, found Gertie buried alive in the basement, pinned by the crumbled chimney. Gertie lost her leg but delivered a healthy baby six months later.

Temperatures in December were below freezing. Survivors began to erect makeshift tents next to the piles of rubble that had been their homes. In time, construction crews from another province built temporary rows of attached homes. Halifax was slow to recover. Collectively, too many lives were lost, some simply vanished to dust, the survivors became the walking wounded.

My grandfather never told us about this explosion he had survived, never mentioned the loss he suffered. Only as an adult did I learn about it and finally understand his confusion on the day his home exploded forty years later—almost to the day. While sitting in the ambulance as a little girl, I had no idea that I was watching my grandfather relive his trauma before me. For the second time in his life, he had survived an explosion and watched his home burn to the ground.

Five years after the Halifax explosion, my grandfather, at eighteen, stuffed a small canvas bag with all he had, placed a few coins in his pocket, and said goodbye to his father and siblings. He climbed onto a railcar headed to Detroit,

Michigan. He had heard Detroit's auto industry was booming and offering steady work. He wanted a fresh start away from the looming collateral damage of the explosion, both seen and unseen. He arrived in 1922, rented a small room in a boarding house, and secured a factory job with Chrysler Corporation, where he remained an employee for forty-two years.

Soon after he arrived in Detroit, he fell deeply in love with a waitress at the corner café. She was a recent transplant herself, from rural Arkansas, and always displayed a fresh flower in her hair. The shared hope for a better life sprouted between them. The Yankee and the southerner soon married and gave birth to my father.

My grandfather sweated daily in the automobile factory, saved every penny he could, and in 1954 the couple purchased a new two-bedroom, one-bath home in East Detroit. My grandfather was living the American Dream.

Grandpa rarely spoke of his childhood, his family in Canada, or his emotions. Every few years his brother, Clifford, and his wife, Mary, and their young children, Heather and Brian, would visit from Nova Scotia. They sat in the garden sipping Grandma's famous lemonade or enjoying a Stroh's beer while catching up on the family. There was never any mention of the explosion.

Grandpa was the patriarch of our immediate family, a strong Scotsman with great pride, work ethic, and conviction. He worked five days a week, 7:00 a.m. to 3:00 p.m., and polished his shoes every morning before work. He ate liverwurst or baloney sandwiches carefully made by Grandma and placed in his lunch box. My grandparents ate fish on Fridays and cherished our Sunday family dinners at their home.

Grandpa bought a new Chrysler car every two years and always kept his garage immaculate. He placed nails, screws, and bolts in separate clear jars and nailed the lids above his work bench, like specimens screwed to the ceiling. If you needed any hardware or a toy fixed, he had the tools. Nothing was out of order ever. He could fix everything, except on that Sunday.

> *Family history can be a source of strength if we have the courage to look behind us.*

In hard times, when my own family struggled to put food on the table, my grandfather would quietly slip through our back door and place bags full of groceries on the kitchen counter. He never shamed my parents for not being able to provide, never made judgments or comments.

My grandpa had an extremely dry sense of humor and a gift for making up limericks and rhyming songs that involved one of the kids' names. "Lesia Lu lost her shoe and stepped on a blueberry pie / When her toes turned blue, she didn't know what to do / So she sat over there and cried!" The words always involved an element of truth and something we did or liked, and he'd sing the lyrics as he strolled by, and we giggled. When he walked, he liked to jingle the coins in his pocket.

When we kids slept overnight at their house, a rare and special occasion, my grandmother bathed us, powdered us down, helped us into our PJs, and tucked us in. My grandpa then came to wiggle our toes before he said good night and shut off the light. I felt loved and cared for. On Saturdays, he and my grandma would cash his paycheck, shop at Pete & Franks farmers market for groceries, cut the lawn, tend to the garden, and then clean up for dinner at five o'clock.

His life was predictable. Nothing ever changed in my grandpa's world. I loved that about him. Perhaps he got that way from the severe trauma and loss he endured as a boy. He lived such a controlled life, maybe because he never wanted to risk experiencing such a devastating traumatic event again. It was the opposite of our life at home. Going to my grandparents for dinner on Sunday was a day I could exhale and feel safe, until I was not.

After the accident, my grandparents pleaded to visit me at the hospital. My parents made excuses to delay the shock of my appearance. I wondered why they didn't come see me, and even my siblings were kept away. It's no wonder why there are no mirrors in burn centers. Once out of bed I kept my head down while learning to walk again because I couldn't bear seeing my face in the reflection of windows in the hallway.

After some time, my parents finally brought my grandfather to the hospital. My grandmother was still too distraught to leave our home. When he shuffled to my bedside, he did his best to hold it together, but his stoic face was soaked with tears. My parents kept his visit brief. Witnessing Grandpa broken and distressed outside the ambulance that night had been devastating. Seeing him for the second time, more in control but still distraught, taught me that the best gift I could give him was to be brave.

My grandfather and I never spoke of the explosion. At times, my thoughts drifted back to my father's outburst in the hospital, telling me how the family was barely hanging on and I was to be strong for everyone else. I had so many questions about what happened, but my mother was busy digging holes to bury the pain while trying to keep the family together. My father made his position clear to me for years: "Lesia, I can't talk about the explosion, because I will cry, and if I cry, I'll never stop." I learned to act strong, be strong, for the family. It was easier. If I acted strong, so would everyone else. The victims of trauma carry the power. I was determined to use mine for good.

The greater-than-normal chaos at my house from calls to insurance companies and lawyers and from concerned friends and family delayed my grandparents' recovery. My father moved them to a modest two-story home on a canal a few miles away. They couldn't climb stairs and didn't know how to swim, but my father swung a deal, and my grandparents could finally start to find peace and create order in their lives again. They had nothing left from the fire but a broken, wounded family and a small check from the insurance company. Yet, they were grateful we were all alive.

As they were getting settled, I was shuffled to various plastic surgeons to be examined, stared at, and photographed while I listened to conversations about how to fix my face. I believed no doctor could fix my face. I often heard my father on the phone with yet another surgeon (or lawyer), "Are you the best? I want the best for my daughter! Who is the best plastic surgeon and lawyer alive today?" I'd sit slumped in the background rolling my eyes. Our electricity was often shut off due to nonpayment, and my father was on the hunt for the best surgeon. Who was going to pay for all this care?

I ended up in Dr. Reed Dingman's office at the University of Michigan. I knew he was important because he led the charge through the crowded hallways with several doctors in tow. He entered the room where I sat on the gurney wearing a loose cotton sheet with holes for arms. All of them in starched white coats, along with the token cameraman, squeezed in to get a closer look. At the end of the exam, Dr. Dingman gently took my rebandaged hand and walked me across the hall into his office of dark-paneled walls covered from floor to ceiling in certificates and awards. My father was close behind with a crack in his side smile and a clip in his step.

"Have a seat here," Dr. Dingman said. "I'm going to call my colleague Dr. Ralph Millard in Miami." As the phone was ringing, he pulled the receiver from his ear and mouthed to my father, "Can you get Lesia to Miami?" I sat numb, listening to another discussion about me as though I were not present. Yet, little did I know at the time I was being carefully handed from one legend to another in the world of reconstructive surgery. My father knew it.

Nine months after the explosion and not long after my visit to Dr. Dingman, my father announced he was moving the family to Fort Lauderdale, Florida, to make a fresh start, as he put it. The additional purpose of the move was to put me closer to my new reconstructive surgeon, Dr. Millard, the successful result of my father's search for the best surgeon. My father sold our nightclub in Detroit and bought us a home on a canal near the beach. My two siblings and I and our parents lived in the main house, and six months later when my grandpa retired, he and my grandma moved from Detroit to Fort Lauderdale into the one-bedroom apartment above our main house. My two older siblings had married and lived nearby. We were one big, happy, wounded family, barely holding on.

When we learn that tears reflect strength, our rivers will overflow with compassion.

I went through a series of reconstructive surgeries after my grandparents moved in, and I could see the agony in my grandpa's face each time I returned from surgery with my face covered in bandages. His limericks became rare; the few coins in his pocket remained silent. Today, I think how my grandpa must have been buried in shock, wrestling with two explosions in his lifetime and never talking about either one.

My grandmother was more dramatic in her response to the explosion. When we were out in public together, inevitably someone would stare at me. She'd start to cry and in her thick Arkansas accent say, "Look here at my poor baby, her face all burned up." Then she'd pull up my shirt to show my other scars, and weep. "My house burned down . . . I lost everything."

When this happened, I'd pretend I was fine, try to minimize her meltdown, and search for my grandpa on the other side of the store to come rescue us. It was always a struggle when Grandma joined us to run an errand. After a simple trip to the store, I'd come home, collapse on my bed, cry silent tears, and vow to never leave the house again.

Going out in public with just Grandpa was different. When curious people who attempted to stare at me saw his stone face and clenched fist at his side, they turned and bolted. I felt protected. Grandpa and I celebrated our birthdays together because they were only one day apart. We'd laugh when by accident I'd rip open a gift that clearly belonged to him, giggling from embarrassment over a package of boxer shorts.

I took his cue to be strong and silent, but I also learned that silent wounds weaken the heart. My grandfather suffered and survived a few heart attacks while we lived together in Fort Lauderdale. When my parents divorced three years later, he and my grandmother moved to Arkansas to be closer to her family. He died one year later at sixty-eight. I was fourteen years old when he died. It wasn't until well after he passed that I got to know about his buried pain.

My grandmother never learned how to drive or write a check. Nine months after my grandfather died, she flew to Fort Lauderdale with little notice and we all went to dinner together. I tucked her into bed and kissed her good night. After I left the room, she swallowed a handful of pills. I found her dead in the morning.

My grandparents were never the same after the explosion. I know if they had received professional help with their grief, if those were times when that was acceptable, their sunset years would've had a little more sunshine.

Losing my childhood that snowy afternoon in Detroit put me on a difficult path with unknown curves. I was too vulnerable both physically and mentally to take people at their face value, so I developed an ability to identify people who were good for me and avoid the others. I figured out how to read the room at a young age.

My father was a good teacher. He could see beyond what people presented to him, perhaps because he had many faces himself. When we visited each other after an extensive abstence period, the first thing he did was put his hands on my shoulders and look straight into my eyes for what seemed like an awkwardly long time and say, "First, I need to really see you." I thought this was just a silly greeting, but then I started to do the same to him—I'd look into his eyes to see if he was okay, too.

By paying attention to what was happening around me at all times, I enhanced my intuition and learned to trust my gut. This has served me well. The downside was if I looked too closely at people, I felt their pain.

Grandparents on their porch, a year before the explosion

Explosion Echo 35

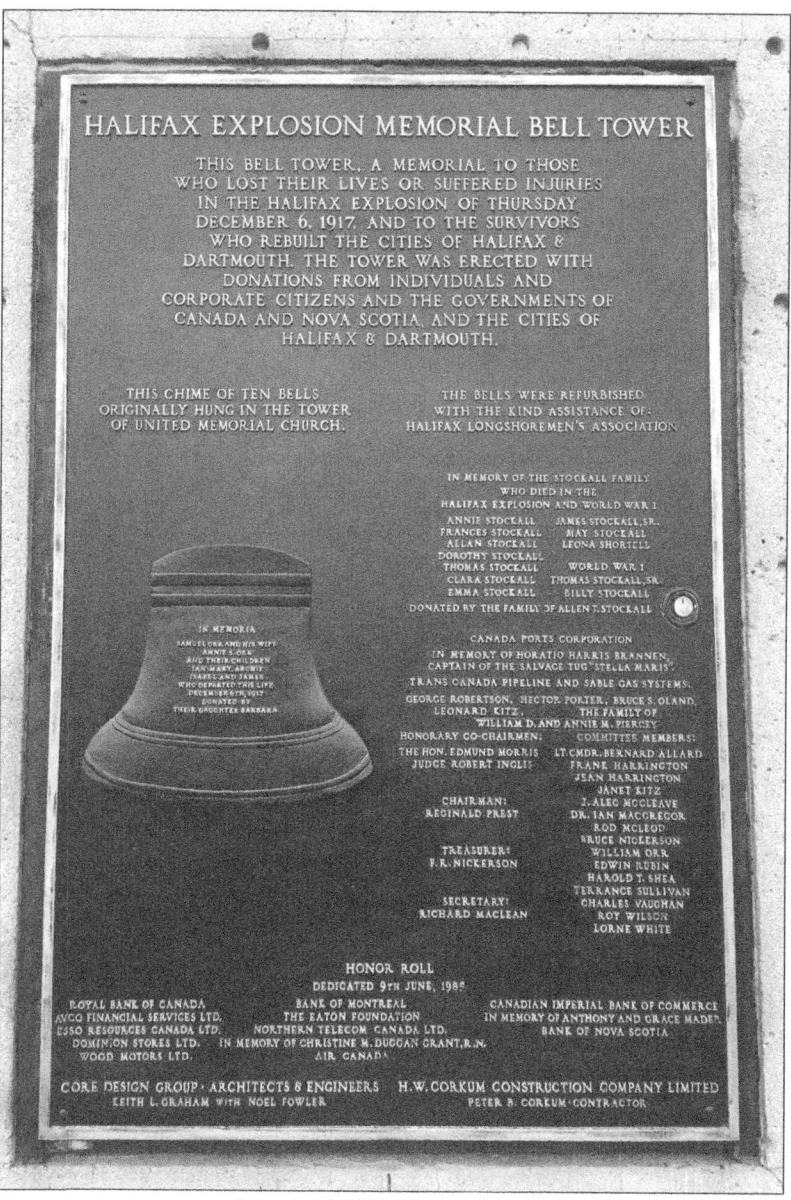

Memorial of Halifax explosion

D. Ralph Millard, M.D., F.A.C.S., Hon. F.R.C.S. Ed., Hon. F.R.C.S. Eng., O.D. Ja
Light-Millard Professor & Chairman Emeritus
The Division of Plastic Surgery, University of Miami School of Medicine

February 14, 2007

Lesia Cartelli
Angel Faces
P.O. Box 235538
Encinitas, CA 92023-5538

Dear Lesia,

I am impressed with the remarkable work you are doing for the facial injured patients.

Keep up the great work!!

Love,

Ralph

D. Ralph Millard, MD

3
"Katie, Breathe"

*Situations are often never as they first appear.
They are laced with our own experiences, judgments,
fears, and values. Stepping back from a situation,
changing your lens, often brings clarity and truth.*

My father called me "the eyes 'n' ears of the world" because I rarely missed the depth around me. I noticed people's reactions and felt their energy. I could often predict what would happen next. But, like everyone else, I also had to learn the hard lesson that all is not always as it appears.

It takes life experience to know when to step in and out of situations and when to stay away from drama altogether. Given our own biases and experiences, it requires courage to stay open to people and opportunities, to trust gingerly.

I'm not a controlling person, and not interested nor qualified to be general manager of the universe, but I will step in when I see someone overwhelmed and know a simple helping hand will make a difference. Sometimes people need to go through their painful process alone; other times, they need help—a lot of help.

Bruce and I arrived at the San Diego airport to begin a quiet romantic weekend to celebrate our fifth wedding anniversary. We were flying to Portland, Oregon, to a cozy creekside cabin tucked in the forest on Mt. Hood.

Two months prior, on September 11, 2001, our world and the security of our country fractured. The airport was a calm and eerily quiet place for a Friday evening. Those of us who were brave enough to fly sported wide eyes and folded arms, looking defensive and wary.

We stood patiently at the security checkpoint, waiting for the only two passengers in front of us to get organized. I watched carefully as they tossed their belongings onto the rolling belt for screening. They were traveling with various pieces of odd luggage, including a Styrofoam cooler and a homemade cardboard box containing an animal I couldn't identify, all while pushing a wheelchair piled high with Mexican blankets. The couple looked in their mid-thirties. She seemed drained; he acted aloof. As I looked closer at the wheelchair, I saw the eyes of a frail old lady peering back at me. Through the tattered threads of the blankets, our eyes locked.

The man held the Styrofoam cooler whose lid kept popping off and sailing to the ground. Bruce picked up the lid and made eye contact with the man as he placed it back on the cooler, receiving a slight smile and nod of gratitude. The woman handed the cardboard box to a security agent. He peeked inside, smiled, and handed the box to another down the row of newly hired security officers. I could hear whimpering coming from the box.

I tried to stay open to a situation I knew nothing about. But my judgment surfaced, and my patience waned. *Good grief!* I thought. *What the hell is happening here? Why would people travel with all this crap: an overstuffed cooler, animals cramped in a makeshift box, and piles of Mexican-type blankets?*

As the woman continued to offload her belongings onto the X-ray belt, her companion let the agents inspect the contents of the Styrofoam cooler; the lid had fallen off again and was now split in half. The agents all wore an expression of compassion. I was lost. "What's in the box?" I mouthed to Bruce.

> *Moving away from assumptions and judgment often brings miracles before our eyes. The key is to stay humble.*

Once the family in front of us finally cleared out, Bruce and I sailed through security, except for the bottle of water he left in his backpack. Busted. The new rules and regulations for flying were still being decided on a national level.

We ended up at the same gate as the mystery family, both of us on the flight to Portland. As I imagined various scenarios, Bruce's phone rang. It was Bobby, his lifelong friend from elementary school. Bruce answered and headed to a quiet area away from the yelping and grunting coming from the family's cardboard box.

I sat close by, intrigued with the situation. *Why didn't they check their luggage, ditch the fragile cooler, leave Granny at home, and let the animal in the box stay in its natural habitat?*

The man set the cooler down and walked off. I watched the overwhelmed, exhausted young woman struggle between keeping the animal quiet and tending to Granny in the wheelchair. She needed some relief.

"How can I help you?" I asked quietly. She looked at me with a blank, watery stare. "Why don't I tend to what's in the box?" I looked in the box and discovered two tiny, sand-colored puppies engaged in a wrestling match. They had no water and were saturated in pee and poo. I lifted the pups to calm them and nearly gagged at their odor. A stinky puppy? I never knew there was such a thing.

This situation looked like a complicated mess. My first thought was, I just want to bathe the puppies quickly and return them. We would be boarding soon and on our way to a romantic weekend.

The woman sank back into her seat, and her eyes flooded with tears. I held the puppies and moved closer to her. My compassion kicked in and obliterated any remaining judgment. I pinned the puppies to my chest with one arm, while holding my breath, and I laid my free hand on her knee. "So, what's going on?"

Elaine explained that her twelve-year-old daughter, Katie, was in the wheelchair and in the final stages of brain cancer. The aloof gentleman was Katie's father, who had been estranged from them for the past decade. She and Katie were returning to Portland from a clinic in Mexico where they had been trying a last-ditch experimental treatment. Just two days ago, Katie's father had heard about his daughter's cancer, flown to Mexico, and found them in Tijuana at the clinic. Elaine had not seen him since he walked out on them when Katie was three years old.

The Styrofoam cooler contained Katie's homeopathic medication. The blankets had come from the nurses in Tijuana to keep Katie's frail body warm. When they drove away from the clinic, Katie had spotted the abandoned puppies on the street and, for the first time in a long time, smiled. The taxi driver made an abrupt turn, picked up the puppies, and stopped by his home for a cardboard box to hold them.

I sat speechless, struggling with the shame of my judgment just minutes ago. In tears, I excused myself from Elaine and, with a click in my step, took the puppies into the women's restroom. I gave them water to drink and a quick bath in the sink, then held them under the blower to dry. I was now soaking wet, but the puppies smelled like puppies, not the city streets.

As I returned to the gate, I could see Bruce sitting at a distance, still on the phone with Bobby. The gate attendant called for passengers needing assistance to preboard. I threw away the soiled newspaper from the box, placed the puppies back in, and helped Elaine and her partner gather their belongings. They went to board.

> *Not all angels have wings. But if you are still, you can recognize them by the feeling in your heart.*

I exhaled into my chair and closed my eyes, a blood-curdling scream came from the gangway.

"Help me! Help me!" Elaine shrieked. "Someone help my baby girl! She's fallen!" I jumped up and called for Bruce. Together we ran down the gangway as he went into emergency-management mode, ordering the gate agent to call 911 and close the doors to the gangway behind us. Katie was folded over on the floor. Bruce rolled her over and began respirations.

I pulled Elaine down to Katie's feet. Together on our knees, each holding a foot, she begged, and we prayed for Katie to wake up, to breathe. "Please! Please! Please, God! Not here, not now, not here," Elaine pleaded. She went from whimpering to wailing and back again—a mother's love in its rawest form.

I looked up and saw the flight crew from our Alaska Airlines plane standing behind Bruce in disbelief as he continued lifesaving respirations. The airplane's captain emerged with oxygen. Katie had soiled herself, and her skin had turned the creepiest dull gray hue I'd ever seen on a live person.

As I watched this little girl die, her mother sobbing in my arms, her hot tears pouring down my chest, I worried for my husband. Who would tap him on his shoulder and tell him to stop life-saving efforts, because we all knew she was gone? Not me. Bruce would never stop. I knew this about him. I had to let his training and his heart be his guide. My prayers were now for my husband. Katie was clearly gone.

Bruce placed the oxygen canula into her nose and continued respirations. Time seemed to stop. He then drew a deep breath and blurted out, "She's pinking up!" We all continued to pray, Elaine begging God for Katie's life. The pink tone in her skin began to cover her entire body. She responded to Bruce's respirations first by moving her hands, then her feet. Bruce paused and slightly raised her head as she made little coughs. The captain, his chin quivering, held hands with the flight attendants by his side. Tears fell like rain in the gangway.

There is a window near death when the light in the room becomes a golden glow. God is present, and the angels have descended. This is when heavenly decisions are made. As we worked in that golden light, a loud bang sounded on the exit door of the gangway to the tarmac. "San Diego Fire Department! Open up!"

The flight attendant opened the door to find paramedics with equipment in hand standing in the pouring rain. They pushed by the flight crew and dropped to their knees next to Bruce, who was still on the floor cradling Katie's head in his hands. Shocked at recognizing Bruce from the fire department, the paramedic tapped Bruce's shoulder. "Hey, Chief, we're here now. We got you . . . we got this."

When Katie collapsed, there was no time to tell the flight crew Bruce was a firefighter and EMT (and now a division chief), nor was there time to tell Bruce about Katie's condition.

Bruce stood up, trying to hide his misty eyes, laid his hand on the medic's back and quietly said, "Thank you." The medics transferred Katie onto their oxygen, strapped her on the gurney, and carried her down the narrow, slippery stairs to the ambulance on the tarmac.

"Where are the puppies now?"

I handed Elaine her handbag, asked for her phone number, and watched her and her companion disappear into the rain to ride in the ambulance with Katie to the children's hospital. I picked up the family's remaining luggage—Styrofoam cooler, blankets, and puppies—and we boarded the plane.

I had never seen anyone come back from "the other side" of life. That little girl had been dead; I felt the stillness in her soul. Elaine's chant rang in my ears for days. "Not here, Lord, not now." My husband never gave up; neither did the angels around her.

I suspected Bruce would crumble from his adrenaline rush. I knew the signs: blank stare, nervous chatter, sweaty hands. I took his face in my hands and told him whatever he wanted from me this weekend, he got.

Passengers at the gate were now boarding. As Bruce and I carried the cooler, blankets, and puppies to our seats, I was reminded of my history of fast karma. Just one hour ago, I stood at the security line, tapping my foot, judging a scene without any knowledge of it.

I took the puppies out of the box, and they fell fast asleep, one in each of our laps. I dropped my head on Bruce's shoulder, and we closed our eyes and joined the puppies in exhaustion. Once we were airborne, the captain announced, "I apologize for the delay; however, we have a hero on board in seat 16A." He went on to say that Bruce saved this little girl's life in the gangway. The entire plane erupted in deafening applause. The flight attendants delivered bottomless champagne to us for the remainder of the flight.

After I gulped down the first glass, I looked at Bruce. "Are you ready for the backstory about Katie?" He set his empty glass down, placed his hand over the puppy, and nodded yes.

As we deplaned in Portland, the managers of Alaska Airlines greeted and escorted us to a private area to thank Bruce for his efforts for their passenger. They explained that Elaine's family had received word of the event, and they were waiting outside security to pick up the luggage and puppies.

It had been an emotional few hours, but what came next pushed us both over the edge. As we rounded the corner past security, there was a floor-to-ceiling glass wall. Behind the glass wall stood a large crowd of people wearing white T-shirts with a picture of Katie on the front: a healthy Katie. They were all holding balloons and signs that read, "Welcome Home, Katie."

After our weekend on Mt. Hood, we had a quiet drive back to Portland. As we entered the city, Bruce asked me to call Elaine and check on Katie. I spoke with a family member to learn that Katie had passed away that morning in the comfort of her mother's arms, in a warm, quiet room.

Months after Katie's death, Elaine wrote a letter to the San Diego Fire Department about Bruce's efforts that day. "He gave me the opportunity to say goodbye to my baby girl in the comfort of a soft place, not the gangway at an airport where many people have trampled,"

> *If you know you have fast karma, you learn quickly to straighten up and fly right.*

Elaine wrote. Bruce's fire department gave him a Heroism Award. We were scheduled to be out of town during the award ceremony. "Do you want me to reschedule our trip so you can be there to accept the award?" I asked.

"No, because she died." He dropped his head.

I reminded him that he gave Elaine the gift of holding her child in comfort and privacy as she passed. It's enough to do what we can with what we have. It's enough to do our best.

The experience with Katie exhausted us both. Even though Bruce had been a firefighter for decades and involved in numerous rescues, this was different. He was not on duty, able to hide his emotions behind a badged uniform, and he had no lifesaving equipment or crew with him (just us weeping, praying women). It all caught him off guard, suddenly holding all the responsibility for this little girl's life.

For me, the experience was Godly. The angels that visited me during my accident seemed to leave a residue of protection in my life. They didn't feel like imaginary friends, or like the friends you phone in a game show if you needed an answer, but rather they were a presence I felt when faced with difficulty. Always there in the background, they stepped closer to me when I needed them. I felt protected on the gangway and sensed wings unfold behind me, a presence that guided me to stay calm and clearheaded for Elaine. It was a familiar feeling from decades ago. I was grateful I hadn't ignored her at the gate, allowing my judgment to take over. When I stay open to what is around me, I may be rewarded with the richness of life.

> *Cleve to the memories of experiences that have brought you light. That light will illuminate inside you and shine a path for others.*

The event also reminded me why I fell in love with Bruce: his ability and courage to do what it takes to save a life, and his compassion for complete strangers. At the Portland airport, after we passed off the puppies, Bruce asked a family member if he could have the enlarged photo of Katie that was pinned to her T-shirt. He rolled up the photo and kept it safe during our travel that weekend. Once home, he put Katie's picture on his wall, where it remained for years.

As time moved forward, our communication with Elaine had waned. Yet that day will always be a gentle reminder to me that there is often more to a situation than the outward appearance.

4
Heart Work

Transforming your pain into purpose is challenging. It requires placing a magnifying glass over the raw areas of your life. However, the reward is an enriched life of love, self-worth, and contentment.

When the girls arrived at the retreats with Angel Faces, they were emotionally and physically shut down. Their hair covered their faces, they wore long sleeves and pants in the hot summer sun, and their eyes darted from the floor off to the side and back again. I recognized their attitude as merely armor they wore to protect themselves from rejection, my motivation to help them heal supercharged. I knew I could get these girls to see how powerful and important they really were underneath the weight of how others viewed and treated them. I felt equipped to teach them about their own resilience. When I look back at the past twenty years of retreats, my heart is full, knowing the mutual agreement between me and my angels is being fulfilled.

My experience of a traumatic injury at such a young age helped me design the framework of the program. I lost relationships, trust, and identity, along with my touchstone—my grandparents' home. I wanted to give the girls what I had learned through facing the challenges of my accident. I wanted them to see that despite the terrible ways the traumatic event changed their lives, there were treasures to be discovered in the aftermath.

Giving to others, besides your children, what you never had is God's love working through you.

I could teach them that it was okay to lose relationships as a result of the accident. People react differently to trauma; throw in shame or guilt, and relationships take a hit—expect it. That doesn't mean they can't be repaired. I wanted the girls to understand that although their trust may be challenged, that doesn't mean they should never trust again. Most importantly, they will thrive and grow when they begin loving and trusting themselves and this will take time.

"I didn't get this far to only get this far." That mantra kept me going. The girls had incredible resilience to survive such traumatic experiences. Now they had to ask themselves what they were going to do with that strength. It was their responsibility to teach others about resilience and faith and to become a beacon of strength that others could look up to.

I often told them, "When you enter a room, people will stare at you anyway. Why not hold your head high and let them stare at your strength and beauty?" Hearing this, some girls would just stand and stare at me, perhaps realizing for the very first time that they are beautiful. The others would roll their eyes and walk away as though I were telling them to go clean up their room.

After my explosion in 1969, therapy was at the bottom of a long list of priorities. My parents were consumed with insurance companies, lawyers, and getting through the day. Those were the times. Communicating with my angels took the place of therapy in my younger years. I was thirty-four when I went to my first session and soaked the sofa with my tears. With my head in trembling hands, I feared I, like my father, would not be able to stop my tears. I wanted to give the girls the benefit of professional help earlier in their healing, before life had a chance to knock them around, rob them of hope, and steal their trust. Putting together a comprehensive mental health component of the retreats was crucial and had to involve a team of skilled licensed professionals.

The mental health team at the retreats has been invaluable in helping the girls work through their trauma and the many ways it manifests. Watching the girls over the years being guided through their past by therapists, I have seen myself. The girls are often stuck in their emotional maturity at the age of their accident. One of the therapists, Shannon Nosenzo, calls this an identity crisis. Shannon says, "Many people who experience a serious trauma report feeling behind in their relationship with themselves, other people, and in their achievements. People often say they feel ten years behind or more." I can relate; gaps of my past seem lost. This identity crisis is common in people with post-traumatic stress disorder. After a traumatic accident, Shannon says, "survival becomes the focus, and their social-emotional learning is paused and sometimes forgotten."

One of our young women, who excelled academically after her accident, went on to earn a master's degree. However, when she returned to the retreat as a mentor, the coping skills of her ten-year-old self emerged when she faced difficulty. Getting unstuck from our identities at the time of the accident can be the work of a lifetime, but the chances of success are far better with professional help. When I see our girls stuck, I get it. It takes work to be free.

Ten years ago, I was fortunate to benefit from breakthrough research utilizing lasers in treating burn scars. I had seen Dr. Jill Waibel, a world-renowned dermatologist and pioneer in the field of lasers, on the *TODAY* show one morning and called her office to schedule a consult. Not long afterward, I found myself in her office preparing for my first laser treatment to minimize the scars on my face. Laying in the treatment room, I fought the memories of being treated after I was burned. It amazes me how quickly we can go back to our younger self of decades ago, vulnerable and powerless. Seeing Dr. Waibel walk into the room, with pearls, heels and her beautiful smile calmed my angst. Yet, as soon as she pierced my skin with the laser, the smell of burning flesh shot me back to 1969 when I lay burning in the basement. Although I was heavily medicated, I knew I was torn between two worlds.

My nine-year-old self needed to escape the smell and burning feeling, but my present-day self knew I chose to be here receiving the best cutting-edge treatment. I winced and whined with a child's voice, crying, and begging someone to help me as I burned. Each time I pleaded

> *We are often emotionally stuck at the age we experienced a severe trauma.*

for Dr. Waibel to stop, she did. She gave me a break, and my husband moved closer to hold my hand. Feeling safe, I passed out again from the medication, but as soon as she touched my face with the laser, I shot awake.

This dance went on for too long. Dr. Waibel empathized with my struggle and shortened the treatment. I slept the entire four-hour drive home. During the following week as I recovered, my husband never mentioned the regression he witnessed.

At my follow-up appointment, Dr. Waibel, in her soft, compassionate way, told me what had happened. "Lesia, I think you have PTSD from the fire that manifested in your cells." I was shocked hearing this, thinking I had already chased down my areas of trauma and beat them into dust. I felt bad for her and all physicians when the patient, in an altered state, begs them to stop treatment. I can imagine many doctors also suffer from PTSD, but in a different way. Who takes care of the treating physicians and all they encounter?

Memories, visions, and events get trapped in our minds and our bodies. As I grew to understand my buried trauma, I understood my grandpa's behavior outside the ambulance. Some residual effects of trauma never fully heal, and we simply must manage it. The good news is there are new treatments for PTSD such as eye movement desensitization and reprocessing (EMDR), which has helped me tremendously.

A traumatic event can also manifest anger. During the retreat, anger and full-blown rage can surface in our girls when we peel back their Band-Aid of survival. The Band-Aid represents all the necessary appointments to schedule and attend, and follow-up treatments like numerous reconstructive surgeries, physical therapy, and endless medications. These obligations required for physical healing often bury the psychological responses. The girls' daily lives become hours of just checking off the boxes for physical care. Meanwhile, their anger percolates. I would feel their rage upon arrival at registration and would know who needed bumpers on their path.

Mix the trauma these girls have suffered with hormones and often overly prescribed pain medications, and the wounds bubble up for action, rarely in a floaty, soft way but in a furious rage. My team and I see this anger manifest in crying and yelling or in the quiet of art therapy. When asked to draw their typical day, even the girls with gentle demeanors smother the canvas in dark lines scribbled in a thousand directions with jagged edges. We have seen girls pick up a stick, wanting to strike anything in their path, to those who sit catatonically, and everything in between.

Acknowledge the anger or sadness you may experience, just don't give it a chair to sit upon.

I tell the girls it's okay to have anger, but don't give it a chair to sit on. Eventually, they can harness their rage into something positive. I get excited when I see them listening. Perhaps for the first time, they understand that anger is normal, and hope could be around the corner. But the choice is theirs to make, and it takes work. A lot of work.

Triggers also present a challenge. Sam, seventeen, was trapped in the classroom with the active shooter who tragically killed seventeen people at Marjory Stoneman Douglas High School in the incident known as the Parkland school shooting. Once her shrapnel wounds had healed, her doctor suggested she go somewhere to rest and hide from the media that was hounding her and other survivors of the high-profile shooting.

We accepted Sam into the retreat just days before the start. I knew I could provide a secluded environment where her identity would be kept private, and she could learn about the impact of trauma. When a girl registers late, this alters transportation, room assignments, Therapeutic Touch schedules, and art project materials. We are a highly personalized retreat, and much of the program content is designed after we receive applications to ensure we address the needs of each girl. When the roster grows, we can't just "put another potato in the soup," as my Polish mother would say.

In Sam's case, she was among the small minority of participants who did not have a severe physical injury from her trauma, so it was important for her to feel she belonged with us. We also knew we would need to address the dynamics of survivor's guilt, as so many of her classmates had died.

On the first day of the retreat, we were ready for Sam, but not her triggers. The girls stay in dorms at a beautiful private school. The airport shuttle arrived on campus and pulled up to the classroom where registration was held. I watched Sam step down from the van, her body trembling from head to toe. She had not been on a school campus since the shooting. It took one of our mental health professionals a long time to calm her down and regulate her breathing. She missed orientation because she was anchored to the bench outside, not capable of stepping into the classroom.

As the week went on, Sam's reaction to the classroom softened, her breath became deep and steady, and her smile widened. I eventually gave her the role of starting the singing bowls before each session. The bowls, widely used in meditations, emanate a beautiful sound vibration that calms the mind and brings the group together to discuss difficult topics such as abuse. Sam's triggers will be with her for a long time; it is my hope she now has the tools to manage her response.

Triggers can last a lifetime. It's been decades since my accident, but today when I hear a crying or screaming child on the next aisle at the grocery store, it pushes me back to the hospital burn ward in bed number six. I'm haunted by the screams of the children from beds one to five, each taken in turn to the tub room across the hall to have their burned, dead skin scrubbed off daily. At the store, I leave my cart to look for the wailing child to assure myself they're not being tortured. Once I see the child is okay, I exhale, return to my cart, and go on with my day. Triggers are real but so are the remedies.

Offering a variety of methods to transform anger or self-soothe when triggers happen is crucial, as we each tend to gravitate to different techniques. And it's important to stay open to the possibility of healing, no matter how silly or foreign an exercise seems. For example, the first day of yoga, the girls always grumble and drag their feet, some wanting to sleep on their mats. But by midweek, they gather in unison, bending, extending, and breathing together, opening themselves up to hope. When we are hungry to heal, feasts come in many flavors.

Teaching the girls how to apply corrective cosmetics is always a hit. When I was thirteen, I unfortunately found myself at a makeup counter with a stunned and newly trained saleswoman who tried to hide my thick, raised scars with what seemed like pancake batter. While shoppers stared from across the store, every splatter she attempted to paste on my face manifested another tear inside me. I slid off the chair, ditching the failed attempt to look normal, ran to the closest restroom, and scrubbed off the paste, unleashing my pent-up tears. I never wanted this to happen to any girl again.

We teach Corrective Cosmetics not as a way to cover up our scars but as a tool to enhance our beauty.

I assembled a team of professional makeup artists to show the girls, in a private setting, tricks and tips for applying special cosmetics. This can be as simple as drawing an eyebrow that was burned off or minimizing redness between surgeries. Our message is clear: we are not covering up our scars; we are enhancing our beauty. Over the years as I watched these special private sessions, my heart rate rose as I recalled that embarrassing day many decades ago. I was determined to create a fun, lighthearted session with music blasting while girls experiment with colorful eye shadows, lip colors, and the latest trends.

In growing and staying current with the times, I periodically asked the girls what changes they would like to see in the program. Early one morning, I received a call from Tara. "Ms. Lesia, you asked what we would like to see changed in the program."

"Yes, Tara, go on."

"Well, umm, a few girls and I were discussing that you taught us we are beautiful in our own way, so could you change the name Corrective Cosmetics to Facial Design because there is nothing for us to correct, right?" Tara asked.

"Oh, Tara! What a brilliant idea! I'll change it today." We design our faces; we choose how to design our lives as well. Over the years, the girls have become my greatest teachers.

I like to push our girls to become the best version of themselves. More times than not, it works, but the process is hard for both me and the girls I push. I find either they are coddled at home, never allowed to make a decision even at seventeen years old, or they are raising themselves, white-knuckling through life's challenges while silently yearning for guidance. I am driven to give them roots and wings, divinely driven.

Remembering the agreement I made with my angels many decades ago, I sometimes feel them working through me, like I'm a glove guided by God. The key is to keep the inside of my glove free of my own fears so there is room for God to direct me. I often don't know what tactic I'll use to help the girls; it just happens.

Lux, from South America, arrived wearing weathered black combat boots, a ruffled skirt that flowed just above her knee, and a white T-shirt with "love me do" painted across the chest. She shuffled up to registration with a guitar slung over her shoulder. In her South American accent, she greeted me with a warm hello. Lux's thick, black, wavy hair covered half her face, anchored intentionally by sunglasses.

Nine months prior, her scorned lover had lured her to a café to talk about the relationship. She told me later that in her gut she had a bad feeling. However, she trusted he wouldn't dare make a scene or hurt her in a public place. As she approached the building, his two accomplices rode by on a bicycle and threw a cup of acid in her face. Lux was badly burned and nearly lost her vision.

On the first night of each retreat, I lie in bed thinking about the girls I met that day and decide which one needs an extra blessing. Once I have the vision, I pray to God for a breakthrough for that girl. Getting Lux to pull her hair back as an act of self-acceptance was my specific prayer that night. On the next day, I casually pulled a bobby pin from my hair, handed it to Lux, and asked her to pin her hair back. "No! No! I look so ugly!" She dropped her head into her hands.

This was going to be a challenge, and I knew I needed to listen to my angels. "Lux, you are so beautiful! The fact that you survived such a horrific attack brings even more light and love to you," I told her. She couldn't see it, and I understood her resistance. The following day, I got the same reaction.

We got to a point where I would simply walk by her and show her the bobby pin. She would smile and, in her heavy accent, say, "No today, Ms. Lesia. Tomorrow. I do it tomorrow!" Tomorrow would come, with the same outcome, but her smiles got bigger. I sat with Lux at lunch and explained that every day she covered her scars in shame, her ex-boyfriend still had control over her.

When I caught her staring at me, I'd show her the bobby pin and raise my brows and mouth. "Giving him *another* day?" She was starting to understand. As long as she covered her face, she was denying herself the love she needed to heal. It was like he was still throwing acid on her. This experience forced me to reflect on how I, too, had given my power away over the years. Yet I was grateful for the people who had followed me around, pushing me to become my best self.

I had to tread carefully and rely on my gut. I didn't want her to start avoiding me. Toward the end of the week, Lux stood among our circle to present her art project. Her sunglasses held her hair in place as usual. I slowly reached up and pulled out a bobby pin from my own snarled mane. She caught my eye, took a deep breath, and threw her sunglasses on the floor, flinging her hair back for all of us to see. "Okay, #&%$ it! No more days. He gets not one more day of me!" The girls roared and cheered. I had no idea that the girls in her dorm were also encouraging her to let his power go. The light in my heart lifted me up to the ceiling.

Breanna was thirteen when she first came to a retreat. As an infant, she was accidentally burned on her face by her mother's curling iron. Raised by a single mom who was often absent, working to provide for the family, Breanna never knew stability. After watching and interacting with her, I could see she was starved for attention and needed direction. Highly emotional, she interrupted conversations, used language that would've had my mouth washed with soap, and exuded too much provocative energy for her age.

Add scars, low self-esteem, and failure in school, and you have a dangerous and volatile recipe for bad boys, drugs, and alcohol. Mid-retreat, I sat with her and explained in my most patient and loving way that if she didn't change her behavior and learn to love herself, she would create a very difficult path for herself. Breanna walked away, shooting me a look over her shoulder. I'm certain her mother had seen that look before, often.

Breanna encountered major struggles through her teenage years and into her early twenties, when she eventually had to crawl out of the hell she made of her life. I received an apology letter from Breanna years later. She wrote that had she listened to my guidance, it would have saved her years of abuse and heartache from poor choices. Stuffed into the envelope with the letter was a wedding invitation. Breanna was finally on the right path, getting married to a lovely man. She now is the mother of a beautiful little girl.

> *Holding on to the hurt someone has given us gives them the power to continue inflicting the hurt upon us.*

After reading Breanna's letter, I invited her to come to the retreat and present her story. It took an enormous amount of courage for Breanna to share her life with a room full of the most vulnerable audience. We never know what we say that just might change the course of someone's life. I'm hopeful one of the girls in the audience made good decisions because of Breanna's story. Our actions and words impact many—just ask George Bailey.

The final night at the retreat is the most powerful. At the barn dance, I really feel the blessings of the week bestowed upon us. One year, as it poured rain outside, the girls line-danced in unison. All from different races, socio-economic backgrounds, education, and origins of trauma, they were woven together by the thread of healing. Hearts were open, social armor chiseled away, and deep wounds beginning to heal.

I stood with Tracy, my cherished longtime volunteer, an occupational therapist from Shriners Children's Hospital, in the massive threshold between the dance floor and the thick wet forest. As the rain bounced off the leaves and misted our faces, I leaned over to her and whispered, "Tracy, can you feel the blessing of this place, and how grateful are we to be here?" Tracy raised her arms up to show me goose bumps. Tears filled our eyes, and she leaned back and nodded yes. As we turned to join the dancing, I caught a glimpse of my angel sitting on a wet leaf, high in the forest, smiling.

The retreats are swathed in challenges and miracles; it's the miracles I cleave to. When you bring adolescent girls and young women, disfigured by a traumatic event, together for one week of intensive therapeutic work, drama is never far away. Yet the ground is fertile for miracles. I have seen drama surface and sink in the same hour, but the bond between the girls lasts for life. Transforming trauma into treasure has given me serenity and contentment.

I'm often asked, "Do you have children?" There is a silent moment before I answer when the faces of all the girls who have come through the retreats flash before my eyes. "Hundreds. I have hundreds." Sometimes, when I don't want to talk about Angel Faces, I smile and say, "No, no children of my blood." There are times when it's too hard to explain what I've witnessed at the retreat in the depth it deserves. But the girls, through our shared bond of trauma and healing, have become my heart daughters.

My first laser with Dr. Jill Waibel

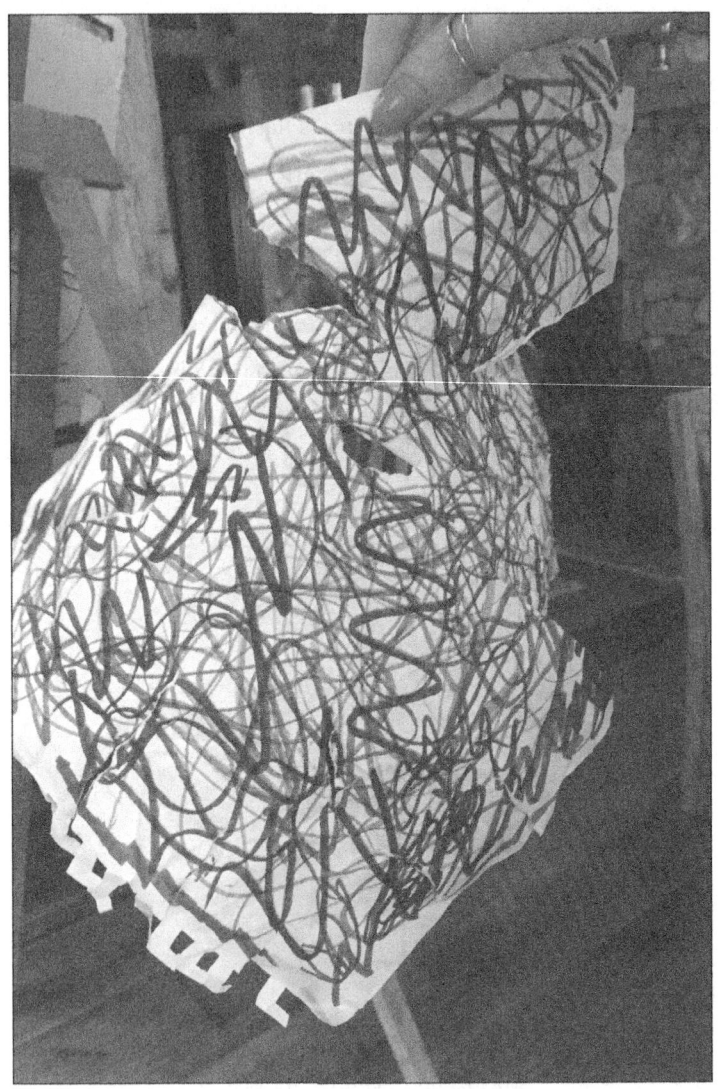

Angel Faces participant, drawing her emotional state

5
Two Days in December

Encouraging yourself to find treasures within a traumatic event can leave you dripping in life's jewels of love and peace. Understanding that the stranger next to you may need jewels, too, is the height of compassion.

The trauma of the Halifax Harbor explosion in 1917 and the loss of so many family members left holes in the hearts of those who remained. A numbness emerged among the surviving community, and the collective memory was largely suppressed. After the first anniversary, the city stopped commemorating the explosion for decades. The second official commemoration did not take place until the fiftieth anniversary in 1967, and after that, the activities stopped again.

In 2011, my sister Cindy visited Nova Scotia and returned with endless stories of our grandfather's life, our Canadian family, and the Halifax explosion. "Explosion? What explosion?" I asked. I was intrigued as Cindy shared what she learned of our grandfather's childhood and the extended family we hardly knew. She gave me a captivating book called *Too Many to Mourn* by James and Rowena Mahar. With every page, the fabric of memories from my own explosion became frayed; loose threads began to show.

Cindy is my adventurous sister. She's not afraid to acknowledge pain and is always ready for a truthful conversation. We travel, shop, eat, hike, and play well together. We often get into uncontrolled fits of belly laughter. She drives like Mr. Magoo, a half-blind cartoon character from our childhood. She once drove so close to a street sweeper I thought it would swipe her car clean.

Cindy told me the one-hundredth anniversary of the Halifax explosion was approaching and asked if I wanted to go to the memorial ceremony in Nova Scotia. "Sure, why not!" I said. We booked four tickets to include our husbands. I was eager for the adventure, the cold weather, old fishing towns, and cool architecture. A bonus would be meeting distant family members and hopefully hearing a few whaling tales. It should be fun, I thought. I knew we were going to attend the memorial of an explosion, but I didn't give it a lot of energy. I was unprepared for what I would experience.

> *Pain is pain, love is love. Regardless of the depth, it is never to be compared but honored.*

As we strolled streets where my grandpa grew up, I struggled to contain the groundswell of emotion. With my vision cloudy, trying to focus through the tears, I felt increasingly dizzy walking the quiet neighborhood where his family's house once stood, where the explosion took the lives of my great-grandmother and great-aunt and several other family members.

Later that night, my newfound family hosted a delicious potluck, their arms enveloping us with heartfelt welcomes and familiar mannerisms. Tears sprang to my eyes when my uncle Brian, my grandpa's nephew and his doppelganger, broke out into a funny limerick. Moments later, another cousin walked by jingling his coins. I felt swallowed up in a time warp, like Grandpa would walk through the door any minute. In all the laughter of being together, I felt the unspoken bond of pain. We talked of family history, the Halifax explosion, and the resiliency our ancestors needed to survive.

None of the family members that evening were alive during the explosion, but in these discussions, I learned that pain is felt through generations. When family members shared stories, a solemn hush came over the room, occasionally sliced by a moment of dry humor. We were the first and second generations after the explosion, our sadness came from hearing how our parents and grandparents struggled with the loss and haunting memories. I had nothing to add, but I understood. I had my own haunting memories of surviving an explosion with Grandpa. I felt a part of this family, and I loved them for it.

I was deeply moved when a distant cousin, Dave, the family historian, pulled out a large book he created of our entire family history. I turned a page to find brochures and awards about Angel Faces. All these years they knew of us, we knew little of them. When I crawled into bed that first night in Halifax, I felt tremendous sadness for my grandfather. He must have been in so much pain to leave behind his loving and supportive kin.

The Halifax explosion must have hurt my grandfather deeply to leave behind the remainder of his loving and supportive family.

The next morning, the anniversary ceremony was to take place on a grassy mound at Fort Needham Memorial Park, which overlooks the harbor and the area devastated by the blast. I woke with a sting in my heart. It was extremely cold outside with freezing rain. Feeling prepared for the weather in my goose down coat with matching hat and gloves, however, I soon realized I was not prepared for the emotional swell of the day.

The crowd of a few hundred ancestors, including my Halifax family, my sister and me, and our spouses, nestled together in the sleet at the ceremony. We were surrounded by the Halifax Regional Police, Canadian Army, Royal Canadian Navy, Royal Canadian Air Force, Mounties, firefighters, dignitaries, and even a one-hundred-year-old civilian who was ten days old when the explosion happened.

As the bagpipers played, my sister and I, along with our cousins, Heather and her daughter, Angela, rounded the large monument to lay a wreath with our family name. When I saw the names of my deceased family members chiseled into the monument, a cut marked my heart. The memories of my own explosion were rising within me. I was grateful for the storm so no one could decipher between my running tears and raindrops.

Nova Scotia premier Stephen McNeil spoke about the determination of those who survived: "Let's think about the positivity, let's think about what we built, what they began to build, and what you and so many other Nova Scotians continue to build upon over these one hundred years."

All I could think about was my grandpa. I visualized him boarding the train to Detroit, working hard all those years to build a better life, only to see his own home engulfed in flames. The memory of sitting on the gurney with my skin peeling in sheets while Grandpa, a strong man in body and mind, became scared and confused had new meaning for me now. From years of treating our girls at Angel Faces and working with our therapists, I understood that some part of Grandpa was stuck in the trauma of the Halifax explosion. In that ambulance, he reverted to his thirteen-year-old self.

My mind flipped between an imagined memory of December 6, 1917, and the crystal clear horrors of December 7, 1969. Images of the two explosions flooded my brain, both taking place on freezing cold days with the ground covered in snow. I knew that traumatic events affect people differently, and my explosion was very different from the one in Halifax. But I've also learned that pain is pain, and love is love, no matter what the scale. I felt lucky to have survived and was motivated to turn my trauma into treasure by helping others through my work. Helping others was one way to help myself. Yet, I felt like I was on a TV show testing how much can I endure before I crumble in tears.

The next stop to commemorate the anniversary was Halifax Fire Station 4 to honor the firefighters who were killed in the explosion. Having been married to Bruce for more than twenty years, I knew that the fire service memorializes with the utmost pomp and circumstance. They do it best. The bells rang, the bagpipers played hymns, and hundreds

I believe the archbishop recognized I was on the verge of imploding, yet given the crowd around us, he avoided the swell of my squirting tears by asking me an question.

of Nova Scotia firefighters in starched uniforms began to march. None of them so much as flinched despite the horizontal sleet pummeling their faces. Standing next to Bruce, my own personal fire chief, I was at home in these surroundings, yet I felt so alone.

After the fire station ceremony, we walked several blocks to Saint Mary's Cathedral Basilica, where we finally shuffled in out of the cold. Archbishop Anthony Mancini led the mass to honor the historic day. The archbishop said from the pulpit, "No one, and I mean no one, in this room really knows what it is like to go through an explosion with our family."

Part of me wanted to stand up like I won Bingo and shout, "I do! I know what it's like! I'm the only one in here who knows what it's like to survive an explosion with their grandpa!" It was becoming almost unbearable to hold the dam of painful memories. I sunk deeper in the pew and clung to the word of God.

Growing up, my mother rarely stood up to my father when it came to the family's needs. She never told him, "No, we are not moving houses every six months" or "I need money for food and clothing, not another impressive painting on the wall" or "I shouldn't be driving the children around in a hearse or Model T." But when it came to our education, she insisted we all attend private Catholic schools to learn the power of prayer and faith in God. She knew she couldn't give us stability, values, and morals like the nuns could. Paying tuition was a strain every month, but she did it.

As a result, I felt at home in church and was comforted by a closeness to God. On this day, I stared at the altar, gilded props, statues, and the massive cross for strength. I glanced down the pew to see the knees of all my family, side by side, sitting in their own painful imagined memories.

Behind the archbishop, against the altar's back wall, sat a row of priests, one of them a family member by marriage, Father Duncan. The year before, Father Duncan visited San Diego with his brother, my cousin Jake. They came to our house for a spaghetti dinner. I saw Father Duncan look over at us with a gentle smile. *All will be okay,* I told myself. Taking deep breaths, I wondered how much longer I would last before I crumbled.

When the mass ended, I sprang from the pew, wanting to escape the endless sorrow. The sad memories had been gnawing at my soul since I woke up that morning. I needed fresh, cold air to keep me from collapsing with grief for myself and my family.

As I squeezed through the exiting crowd, someone grabbed my arm from behind. "Lesia, come with me. I want to introduce you to the archbishop!" It was Father Duncan. In what felt like my final breath, I was swept down the aisle through the crowd to arrive at the feet of the archbishop, a tall man in pontifical vestments and mitre. I felt five years old. "Archbishop Mancini, this is Lesia. She's part of my family I was telling you about from California." Father Duncan then whispered something to the archbishop, who was surrounded by a crowd of people yearning for his attention.

The archbishop veiled my hands and tilted forward, nearly piercing my hat with the point of his mitre. "Aw, Lesia, now what brings you here to Nova Scotia?" Just as my bucket of tears was set to tumble, spewing snot, makeup, and mascara all over his starched, cream-colored vestments, Cindy and Heather appeared on either side of me, saving the moment by answering his questions. I stood in silence, staring down at his shiny black shoes, wishing he could click them three times and I'd be home. He placed his hand over my head, and I received the blessing I needed. I don't remember much else except the feeling of wanting to crawl into God's arms for a very long nap.

The next day was December 7, the anniversary of my own personal hell and Grandpa's second horrific explosion. Some anniversaries are hard; others I sail through. I try to do something good for my soul. I'll book a self-care treatment, a massage or manicure, spend time alone with God, or enjoy a hike in nature. Despite my plan, some years self-pity mows over; other anniversaries I'm full of gratitude for all the blessings I've received and the beautiful people in my life that I would not have met if I wasn't severely injured. On this morning in Halifax, I was numb from my toes to my fingers, including my heart. I needed a normal day with no acknowledgment of what happened when I was nine. Yesterday was too rough.

We spent the day touring the picturesque coast of Nova Scotia with my newfound family, filling my heart and eyes with beauty. Peggy's Cove, a famous lighthouse, stood on a rock foundation. Her exterior was tall and white, and her purpose was to guide the sailors safely home. That day I yearned for my own lighthouse. The next morning, Bruce and I packed the rental car and headed back to Maine for our flight home. Throughout the drive I felt the familiar bulge of tears swelling inside me again. This trip had blindsided me. I never heard any whaling stories and paid no attention to the architecture. What I did was gain a greater love and understanding of my grandpa and deep affection for my Halifax relatives.

At first, I wondered how a man could appear so strong despite how wounded he had to be inside. I assumed Grandpa buried his pain. But maybe that's wrong. Perhaps he used his childhood pain to create a safe place to live, working hard to purchase the perfect home, keeping his wife happy, and enjoying his grandchildren. Maybe that explosion that killed his mother and siblings resulted in his renowned stability and resilience.

I like to think Grandpa created a good life not by white-knuckling through every day but by choosing to live a life of peace and gratitude. He didn't bury his woes in alcohol or become chronically jobless or homeless. Perhaps he had dealt with his agony after the explosion and made a conscious effort to leave it behind in Halifax when he came to Detroit. I just wish he and I had talked about the explosion—both of them.

> *How does a man appear so stoic and strong despite the wounds inside?*

Recently, I gave a talk in San Diego about Angel Faces, including a brief background as to why I started the foundation. Afterward, an elderly woman in the audience struggled to stand. She asked, "Before your grandparents passed away, did they know about all the great work you are doing for these girls?" It was a question I had never been asked before. Suddenly, I felt my grandparents' eyes upon me, like two angels cuddled together, smiling at me. Through a swell of rising and unexpected tears, all I could answer was "No." But then I pointed up and smiled. By the decibels of the applause, I believe the audience felt them above as well. They are watching, and I pray I see them again one day.

Al (Cindy's husband), Cindy, me and Heather

Cindy and I at the family gravesite in Halifax

Halifax family

6
Dream Maker

*Timing is everything. It helps if you wear a watch,
know how to tell time, and learn to listen to time.
But more importantly is that you trust the timing
and all it brings.*

Witnessing and working through the collateral damage of the girls' trauma at our retreats takes its toll on me. By the end, I am spent and in need of my own retreat. This year, the day before we departed our idyllic setting in Corona, California, I trudged to the site office to settle the bill and secure our future dates. The lady behind the desk informed me the property was for sale, and no future rental contracts were available.

I was blindsided and crushed. After seven years, we would not be returning to this spot. How would I tell the girls and volunteers we'd lost the facility? In many ways, it was the perfect place for us, nestled among acres of fruit trees and isolated from the public's peering eyes. The property was adjacent to a popular day spa. On Therapeutic Touch Day, our girls simply stepped through a private gate to the spa grounds where a team of masseuses and aestheticians, who volunteered their time for Angel Faces, stood ready to indulge our girls with massages and facials. This was an important part of our program; it eased the girls into the practice of receiving unconditional nurturing while embracing their new bodies. Their shift in acceptance was real.

Despite my exhaustion, I couldn't sleep that night as I wrestled with this news. I had no idea where our future retreats would call home. The next morning, I remembered that I was in the grip of my angels. Losing the facility was unsettling, but it would all work out for our highest good—always does, always will.

The key to serving sad news is to follow up with hope for dessert. The girls had gone home, and the last bin of supplies had been loaded into the trailer. I stood before my tribe of tired and sweaty volunteers. "Ladies, as we drive out of here this morning, leaving another week of witnessing miracles in the moments, take a good look around these beautiful grounds. The property is being sold; we won't be coming back here." In between the moans of disappointment, I continued, "But we will find what we need. I believe this to be true."

I had faith that everything always works out—often better than we imagine—if we get out of God's way and keep working. As I drove home, I flipped between thinking, *We've got to find a better place* and *Maybe we're done*. The Corona facility, while perfect in some ways, had its drawbacks. Its high-desert location brought scorching temperatures. Burn scars and heat don't do well together. Some of our girls have up to 90 percent of their bodies covered in thick molten scars, which have no pores. With their ability to regulate extreme temperatures compromised, the girls overheat easily.

In the following months, we searched Southern California for a new facility.

We found nothing. Either a potential facility was already booked a year in advance, or the facility didn't meet our needs. I couldn't give up. I kept my spiritual seat belt fastened, ready to rumble with the nearby cavalry of angels.

> It's easy to have faith when your health is good, you have money in the bank, and your family is happy and healthy. Faith is required and questioned when life's challenges are overflowing. Ask Job.

At another successful fundraising dinner for Angel Faces at a private home in Encinitas, California, tireless volunteers folded tables, stacked chairs, and returned glasses and cutlery to the caterer's racks. I sat rubbing my feet while the legs of my chair sank into the moist grass. I hoped the remaining few guests claiming their auction items didn't see my exhaustion.

Three young girls from our previous retreats had arrived a few days prior to prepare a presentation for the fundraiser. We spent the time shopping for their dresses, shoes, and earrings, and practicing their presentations. I also took them sightseeing and to ogle the surfers. We discussed life's challenges, and I held their hearts. There was also my own heart to protect and presentation to prepare. It takes a lot for me to be "on," lassoing my passion and cradling the girls' pain while showing my sincere gratitude for generous donors. Thus, I was exhausted before the fundraiser even began.

I saw someone heading my way and struggled to squeeze my swollen foot back into my shoe. As she got closer, her bright aura illuminated. She was young, energetic, and gifted with long, wild hair paired with a smile that lit up the dark night. "Hi. Are you the founder of this organization?" Her eyes sparkled with tears.

"Yes, I am!" I smiled while standing to greet her.

"The love I feel here tonight has touched my heart. I want to be a part of what you are doing. Please, how can I help?"

"I'm sorry, I didn't catch your name," I said.

"It's Johnna!"

Johnna may have been bursting with enthusiasm, but my feet hurt, my hands were pasty from greeting guests, and my dress felt a stitch too tight. These events can drain one's reservoir, and mine was empty. I thanked Johnna for her kind words with the promise of sharing lunch together soon. Something told me I'd never forget her.

A few weeks went by when I found Johnna's name and number on a sticky note among piles of event receipts and auction paperwork. Remembering that opportunities are everywhere if you stay open, I called her up and made a lunch date. I brought my executive director, Elizabeth, to help me get a feel for Johnna and to see what the girl with vibrant aura was all about. We started lunch chatting about the subtleties of San Diego weather while we picked at our salads.

"Lesia, what do you want, what do you need?" Johnna asked. "I don't have any money, but I may have resources to help you."

Pondering what this young woman could offer, I pulled back my arrow and aimed high. "Johnna, I need a large home in a private setting, on a lake, located on the East Coast so we can serve patients who have been treated at the major trauma centers in Boston, New York, and the mid-Atlantic region." This concept rolled off my tongue as though it had been scripted. Perhaps it was—scripted by my angels straight to my tongue.

Elizabeth shot me a perplexed look across the table. This vision was news to her. I continued, "Parents are hesitant to send their daughters, recently released from the hospital after a severe trauma, across the country to California to attend a retreat. Expanding our retreats to the East Coast would allow us to serve more girls." Shooting for the moon when asking for what we need is brave and risky, admittedly with a touch of arrogance, but my request was wrapped in faith.

So we will be holding sessions in a baby Jesus barn?

How can I make this work for my girls?

Johnna raised her eyebrows. "Well, I think I can help you." She went on to explain that her ex-husband's brother had a home on a lake in New Hampshire. Although the contact was no longer related, she felt connected to his family, and they still liked her. I listened with hope but felt doubtful. I'd had too many lunches with potential donors offering resources that, after dessert, shrank into the abyss.

Back at the office, I told Elizabeth I felt hope in my heart for Johnna's mission, but I was only going to hold my breath for thirty days. "I'm praying we will hear back from her. But we need to keep scouting for a location for the next retreat." Elizabeth agreed, and our work continued.

Soon after our lunch, Johnna called and explained she was working on our request. It was now October. Planning for the next retreat, in June, needed to be underway, yet we were still without a home.

Bruce, who retired as a division chief from San Diego's Fire-Rescue Department, now works for a large hotel and hospitality empire as their fire and life safety inspector. It's a post-retirement, part-time job to keep him busy and gives him a sense of being productive. After thirty-six years in the fire service, he has seen enough tragedy. This is a fun encore career working for a corporation known for treating their employees like family, and it involves a lot of travel, which he loves.

Three years prior to meeting Johnna, I accompanied Bruce to his company's Christmas party at a beautiful conference center on the Chesapeake Bay in Maryland. With the holiday celebration underway, I slipped away from the conversations, peeked into adjacent rooms, then stepped outside to see the grounds. At every turn, I thought, *What a perfect place to host a retreat for Angel Faces!*

During dessert, I shared my thoughts with Bruce. He tilted his head toward a table across the room. "Lesia, my bosses are at that table. Go tell them what type of work you do and inquire about the use of this location for your next retreat!" Bruce was always direct in his delivery. That is not my style.

"No, Bruce," I whispered. "You know I don't operate that way. If this company was meant to support Angel Faces, then it will happen because of our mission, not by leveraging your position with the company."

"Well, you're missing an obvious opportunity," he razzed.

"I just don't want to jeopardize your position. If God wants us to gain support for Angel Faces from your employer, that will happen. Somehow," I murmured. As we left the party, I snatched a glossy trifold brochure of the facility.

Manifestation is planting a powerful seed, then watering the seed with vision, hope, and hard work. I stuffed the brochure into my luggage for our cross-country flight home, then carefully placed it in a special box in my office like a sacred scroll.

It was six weeks since our lunch when Johnna called with excitement in her voice. "Lesia, can you get over to the

Chart House restaurant in Cardiff in thirty minutes? I want you to meet someone!" I was grateful I dressed for a meeting I didn't know I was attending.

"Sure. So who am I meeting?" Now my faith was waking up.

"Remember I told you I might have a place for your retreat on the East Coast? You'll be meeting my ex-brother-in-law. He's connected to the place that would be good for a retreat site."

I was beginning to understand that despite her being the "ex" in the family, this girl had a personal power that was intoxicating. How could you not love her? "Okay, great! What's his name?"

"Bob, and he'll meet you there. He's coming from San Diego headed to Orange County. I'll be there, too, but I'll be late."

All this sounded fragmented, but I resolved to stay open to the possibilities. Besides, I love a good adventure. I could hear my angels giggling.

I arrived at the Chart House to an empty parking lot, doors unlocked but the restaurant empty inside. They did not serve between lunch and dinner, but the hostess surfaced and asked if I wanted anything to drink. I declined and waited on a bench just inside the door, watching for a suited man.

Hopefully, he's not frustrated that his ex-sister-in-law obligated him at the last minute.

Many times in the past, I've assumed someone's appearance before seeing them in person. I think we all do it. It's an exercise in visualizing, manifesting, and stereotyping. Not negative or judgmental, for me it's a fun mental game that nurtures my intuition. I'm rarely surprised. Today was different.

> *Faith is when you are presented a gift and you have a sense of what's inside, but no clue how to open the box without a proper tool. So, you search endlessly for the tool, or you create your own.*

The restaurant sits steps from the Pacific Ocean. It was a chilly day, and surfers were riding the glassy swells. The door cracked open, and a young, attractive, athletic-looking man in a navy, North Face puffy jacket slipped inside. I assumed he was a waiter reporting for duty. I looked up, smiled, then looked away. *No, not Bob,* I thought. Bob would be in a suit and tie, wearing polished shoes, oozing some serious business energy.

"Are you Lesia?" the surfer-like guy asked as he ran his fingers through his cropped, gelled hair.

"Bob?" I stood, tipping my head in doubt.

"Yeah, I know. I get that a lot," he smiled. "Let's sit down over here and chat."

Getting right to business, he asked me about Angel Faces. I shared pictures of the girls on my iPad and explained why I started the organization and our mission. He asked me how I knew Johnna and if I knew anything about who he was.

"Um, not really. Johnna shared that you were her ex-brother-in-law, and I should meet you here."

He nodded. "That's how Johnna rolls!" We shared a kind laugh.

He explained who he was and the corporation he was affiliated with in the hospitality industry. As I learned more about the company, my skin tingled. This was the same company that employed my husband. The company I declined to approach at the Christmas party, where I told my husband that if God wanted Angel Faces to get their support, he would make it happen.

With my thoughts swirling, I had a hard time absorbing what Bob was saying next. I couldn't quite believe the coincidence. Bob made it clear that whatever support he and his family might lend Angel Faces would be a personal, in-kind donation from his family, not the corporation. This was to be looked upon as a private, anonymous donation.

I had to stop him. "Bob, I have something to share with you." My voice sank. "My husband works for your corporation." I was prepared for rejection, thinking Bruce's link to the company would complicate matters. I would express my gratitude for his time and say goodbye.

"Wait, your husband works for us? What does he do?" I shared Bruce's title and how much he loved his work. "Lesia, why haven't you gone to the corporation to request funding for Angel Faces?"

I told him about the Christmas party three years ago on the Chesapeake Bay and the conversation with my husband over dessert. "I declined my husband's suggestion to approach his bosses." As I reached for my keys, he put his hand up.

"Wait, Lesia, that is really cool!"

"So, the meeting isn't over?" I squinted.

"Please, sit down. I'm impressed with your principles. Tell me more about your program." No longer just a coincidence, this now felt like divine intervention—a seed planted three years ago in Maryland sprouting a miracle in San Diego. Bob and I spent another thirty minutes talking before Johnna blew through the door.

"I'm sorry I'm late. What a day I've had!" She exhaled, blowing pixie dust into the air. "I'm so glad you two could meet. So, how's it going?" She beamed.

As Bob and Johnna caught up on their personal lives, below the table my foot felt stuck. I tugged, and the sole of my boot ripped off, stuck under the table's center post. Good grief. I tried to hide my struggle, but Bob looked down, and I feared he saw the bottom of my shoe half gone. I wondered if he would ask why I didn't buy new boots. "Nonprofit salary" would've been my reply. To his credit, he didn't say a word.

The talk returned to Angel Faces, and I had a lot of questions for Bob about his family's home in New Hampshire. There are many important negotiables and non-negotiables in choosing a facility for a successful retreat. Bob mentioned a boathouse and a barn as potential sites for yoga and other programs, and I was skeptical. "Do you mean like a baby Jesus barn? We'll have forty people. Some of the girls are still in bandages."

Bob laughed. "Lesia, I think you really must see for yourself what we have to offer you so you can determine if it'll work for your needs. It's hard to explain. I'll get with my family and be in touch."

We said our goodbyes, and I drove home trying to process what had just happened. With each corner, I could feel God's grip. I was not to worry.

Six weeks later, I found myself deplaning at Boston Logan International Airport in the dead of winter with Piper, my logistics volunteer. Piper was a captain with the San Diego Fire and Life Safety Department and my true north when it came to friendship and leadership. We met during a peer support program we were designing for the fire department. In the midst of the rollout, the 9/11 attack happened, and that bonded us. Her planning skills and mind for logistical details are stellar. Her humor brings light to the most somber moments, and her dental floss berry ice cubes can change your life. She has been a volunteer with Angel Faces since the start.

We drove two hours on icy roads into New Hampshire, arriving at a beautiful inn located in the center of the town of Wolfeboro, which looked like a Hallmark movie set. It was February in New England. Footprints of those who were brave enough to venture out pocked the deep snow. Everything was pristine with a gentle, quiet vibe. We checked into the inn and poured ourselves hot teas. I collapsed into bed with the feeling that I was home in a place I had never been.

Twenty years ago, I had made a list of the things I wanted to do before I died. Living in New England made the top ten. Experiencing this town under a blanket of bright, blinding snow, I was convinced my list needed to move from a dusty box under my bed to my refrigerator as soon as I returned to San Diego.

The following morning, Bob's family met us in the lobby. Bob was not with the group, but his wife, Jen, was the first to greet us. *She's just as radiant as Johnna,* I thought. With her was Jen's sister, Ashley, and her husband, Spencer. Their beauty and warmth on such a frosty day was welcoming. I felt immediately like I had known these people my whole life. We piled into our separate vehicles, Piper at the wheel of our rental SUV and the family in their vehicle, and we followed them a few miles out of town. We turned down a long, narrow private road flanked on each side by a thick forest blanketed with snow. Pristine, angelic light beams shot through the statuesque trees. Hints of emerald pine and fir tree branches poked through the snow. Our tires on the powdery snow made a scrunching sound. This was the closest thing to heaven I could imagine.

The expansive, stately home, the picture of New England charm with a cedar shingle roof and white trim, sat at the edge of the lake with rows of windows to take in the view. The lake was inches from the house—so private our girls could wear swimsuits without worry of their scars being stared upon. Even though it was all frozen over, I had visions of us swimming in the summer, finally being able to exhale from our trauma in privacy.

I was so caught up in the magic of this enormously kind and generous family, and the magnificence of the environment, that I diminished the obvious logistical challenges of hosting a retreat here. The home had beautifully decorated bedrooms, but we were several beds and bathrooms short for a group of thirty to forty women. The newly renovated interior featured everything luxury, elegant, and perishable. It wasn't suitable for a big group of teenagers—not if I wanted this relationship to grow.

The barn sat on a hill in the distance. Jen started to climb through the snow, stomping her boots to pave a path. "Just follow my steps, Lesia. I'll lead the way." When we reached the barn, I felt as if I were standing in a wooden structure as old as time, constructed over centuries with the finest skilled labor and painstakingly maintained. Tree trunks rose from the floor to the second-story ceiling like ancestors watching over their people. I could almost hear horse hooves clip-clopping over the wood floors, carrying royalty through the massive glass double doors. "Barn" seemed like the wrong word for a building so enormous and majestic. *This is crazy*, I whispered to myself.

To go from a facility in Corona in the high, dusty desert to this gorgeous private site in a forest was one thing. But to be closer to the major trauma centers that treated our girls was a miracle. It was a clear reminder to me that my angels kept their word. The harder I worked, the more present they were.

"Do you think this will work for your program?" Spencer asked.

"Yes." I nodded, tears of gratitude floating in my bottom lids. As we wrapped up the tour, the family led us on a snowy trek around the property. It was so quiet you could nearly hear the pads on the bunnies' feet gracing the snow. I was grateful I had purchased new boots for the trip, replacing the pair with the sole wrapped around the table's pole.

It had been a long day for us all—the family also had traveled from California and Boston—so we agreed to wrap up and meet the following morning for breakfast to discuss ideas and possibilities.

As we drove out of the forest, I was elated at the thought of hosting a retreat here in the summer—the privacy of the grounds, the lake, comfortable areas for my girls to feel safe to work on their trauma and begin to heal. Piper thought differently. She hit me with the hard truth as she maneuvered on the icy roads. "Lesia, you know this whole setup won't work for us to run a successful retreat, right? You need to tell the family tomorrow morning. It's such a generous offer and a tranquil setting, but it's not going to work!"

I looked at Piper with disbelief and trepidation. "What? We *must* make it work. There's always a way, Piper! We just need to think creatively! We can't give this up. I adore this family, and I love the energy here!"

Piper pulled the SUV over and turned toward me. "Lesia, look, what they are offering does not meet our needs to run a successful retreat. Let's start with feeding the girls and volunteers. Who's going to plan the meals, shop, and meal prep? Did you even see any grocery stores driving in? The kitchen is beautiful but too small for the size of our group. There are only five bathrooms for thirty-plus women, and where will we all sleep with only eight beds? And we are two hours from a major airport! Lesia, I'm sorry, but as your logistics lead, I must tell you it won't work!"

It was the first time Piper and I had come to an impasse. We had been close friends for ten years. I thought she had lost her creative vision; she must have thought I'd lost my mind, period.

We drove back to the inn silently. The tension building between us followed us up the stairs as we retreated to our rooms. We agreed to meet back in the lobby in one hour, each hoping the other would come back to her senses. I lay down for a thirty-minute power nap. I visualized curling up in God's lap. I knew, somehow, that I was not led here to hit a wall.

Downstairs to meet Piper, I sat in an overstuffed chair by the window and stared at a tree covered in snow with one red cardinal perched on the edge of a branch. I thought of my father and how creative he was with visions and possibilities. Red cardinals, many believe, are a symbol of communication from people who have passed on. As I watched the cardinal on the branch, another bird joined in. By the time Piper arrived, the tree was filled with cardinals. This was a powerful sign.

"Come, Piper, let's drive around and check out the beautiful town." I knew something bigger than us was manifesting. Staying open to possibilities seemed my only option.

We loaded into the vehicle, tossing our hats, scarves, and gloves in the backseat as the heater forced more hot air between us. We remained awkwardly silent. I still believed I was correct, but I also trusted Piper's input. As we drove through the small town, I saw a large, snow-covered sign that read, "Brewster Academy, established in 1887." The property had several large, New England Colonial-style buildings that sprawled down to the icy lake dotted with ice fishing huts. "Piper, what is this place? It looks beautiful. Let's check it out!" I could hear Piper's eyes roll, but she pulled into the parking lot..

Our vehicle came to a slippery stop, and we shuffled up an arctic path, like Bambi on ice, following a sign for the office. We pushed through the door and exhaled at the blast of heat inside. "Excuse me," I whispered to the lady tucked behind her desk and buried in a woolen sweater. "We're from California, and we are looking for a place to host a retreat this summer. Is there someone we can talk to?"

A tall, attractive woman popped through another door and, with a thick Australian accent, said, "Sure, mates, come on in!" She introduced herself as Raylene, the director of Brewster's summer programs. *What is the director of summer programs doing here in the dead of winter?* I wondered. *Another God moment, I suspect.*

Piper peppered her with a list of questions around logistics, transportation from the airport, food, facilities, and dormitories. Raylene casually went through Piper's list and had solutions for nearly every concern. They had small buses to pick up their students at several airports; they could certainly pick up our girls. Brewster had a bountiful dining hall with various food stations to feed many people. "What about sleeping arrangements?" asked Piper.

"Yes!" Raylene waved her hand like she was a fairy godmother—poof! "We've got lovely dorms for your girls!" The three of us sat at a small round table in her office, checking off every box required to run a successful retreat. Raylene grabbed her coat, gloves, and scarf. "Come, follow me. I will give you a tour."

We ventured into the flurries of snow to see the campus. Brewster had nearly a half a mile of shoreline on Lake Winnipesaukee, one of the largest and most picturesque lakes in New England. In the summer, this place had to be beautiful. As we toured the campus, Piper peeked over her scarf with watering eyes. "Lesia, two hours ago we were stalled, no answers in sight. Any possibilities lay frozen in those icy waters. Now we have solutions for every challenge! How does this always happen when I'm with you?"

I and my hopes went into overdrive. This option for room and board at Brewster would allow us to use the amazing facilities at the lake house to host programs, if the family agreed.

Our newfound partnership with Brewster was a win for both of us. "June is a quiet month," Raylene explained. "It's after our school year ends and before the summer programs start, so you'll have the campus to yourself, and our chefs would love to cook for you!"

Piper and I went back to the inn, sipped a martini, and relished dinner. I shook my head in amazement. "I think Raylene just saved our friendship."

"You mean Saint Raylene?" Piper raised her glass, and we toasted our potential new retreat site. The energy between us felt amusing and familiar again.

We met the family the following morning for breakfast. I noticed the same light around them that I'd seen in Johnna. As we got settled, the family brought up concerns about the logistical challenges that Piper shared yesterday. Not wanting to dwell on the challenges we all knew existed, I was eager to relay our newfound solutions. "So, you're not going to believe what happened yesterday after we left you!" I cried, nearly leaping from my chair. Jen's eyes grew expansive. I explained how we stumbled upon Brewster Academy, met Raylene, and spent two hours touring the Academy, which offered a remedy for our capacity problems.

When we feel safe, our veil drops and often the surprise of kindness comes rushing in.

I laid out our thoughts: Brewster would provide transportation to and from the airports and during the retreat. They had plenty of dormitories for the girls and a few volunteers, and a large dining hall to feed everyone. My team of therapists and medical staff would stay on your family's private estate, should you allow. The girls would be transported to the property for a daily program in the enormous barn, then return to Brewster for dinner and the evening program."

As I caught my breath to continue, one of the siblings stood. "That's brilliant. Why didn't I think of that!?" Another sprang up and shouted, "I'll pay Brewster's bill for the retreat!" The whole scene was divinely driven. We celebrated over eggs and orange juice while learning more about one another.

The first couple of retreats at Wolfeboro were new territory for us. The tight-knit town's reaction to our girls seemed like an awkward dance where we attempted to find the beat together without music. The girls' injuries are hard to look at, especially when in a group. The damage can be overwhelming. Yet, I think it was the way I tried to protect them from the pain of unwanted stares that may have fed the town's uncertain response. In the beginning, we would walk to the iconic local ice cream shop, Yum Yum, order our cones, and walk back to Brewster enjoying every lick. As time went on, the town greeted us with warm smiles, asked where we were from and how we all knew one another. No mention of scars, trauma, or accidents. I felt safe and began to let the veil drop to encourage the girls to engage in conversations with the locals, answer their questions, and respond to their kindness with kindness.

At a recent retreat, after a hard day of trauma work, we walked to Yum Yum for ice cream, all thirty of us. As I stood in the front courtyard laughing with the girls and licking my favorite cone, chocolate cherry, a gentleman approached me. "I understand you are the leader of this group."

"Yes, that would be me." I smiled.

He threw his arms up in the air. "Well, little lady, we love you being here! Look at this place. You have lit this town up with energy!"

The town still has the Hallmark energy it has held for over two hundred years. Bruce and I stopped in Wolfeboro while enroute to Nova Scotia and stayed at the same inn. I sat staring out the same large window in the lobby. The tree had grown, but no cardinal birds sat on its branches, perhaps because I had already received their message. I was home.

Dream Maker 105

Red cardinals visiting me in Wolfeboro, New Hampshire

7
"Heart in Heaven"

*Truth speaks paramount through
the language of symbolism. Comfort lives
in seeing beyond the obvious shape.*

When I'm consumed by doubt or question what action to take, I try to be still and tune in to my gut. Listening to my angels or God takes enormous stillness and devoted time, but the answer is usually there. Sometimes, though, I can't be still; I'm distracted, or doubts have clouded my clarity. For those times when I'm not still enough, I look outside myself for my angels' guidance, a sign that shows me I'm on the right path and making the best choice. Intuition, changeable and intangible, can be hard to gauge. Tangible signs, on the other hand, are undeniable.

Throughout my adult life, hearts have been the signs that spark insight, reassure me, and give me the courage to follow my instincts. I don't mean the hearts you see on plates, artwork, clothing, or trinkets, but the ones that appear spontaneously in everyday things like a cloud, a baked potato, a stain on a sidewalk, or even a shadow.

The first time a heart appeared in my life as a sign, I was high up in the Sierra Nevada. Kirkwood, California, is a skier's paradise. I had never skied before, but my friend owned a condominium at the resort that he gifted to me during the winter over the years. Driving Highway 88 into Kirkwood opened my heart to serenity. The mere sight of snow brought out a childlike energy in every fiber, and I became giddy with excitement. I convinced my companion to bundle up in the 20-degree weather to make snow angels, venture on a full-moon hike, and go dog-sledding—anything to play in the snow. I was obsessed.

> I've listened to my intuition mumbling to me for years. When I ignored the message in my gut, the situation never turned out well.

Having skied only once before, decades ago, I took a lesson. The following day, as I swooshed down the bunny slope, I looked up and saw a massive heart made of snow. The snow had fallen between boulders on the side of a mountain and gathered into the shape of a perfect heart. At that moment, I had a revelation about my love of snow. I knew why it always seemed to transform me into a kid again.

My accident, at age nine, took place in December in Michigan. After months in the hospital, I was too frail to play in the snow. I could only stare out our picture window at the soft flakes falling as I recovered from my injuries. Nine months later, we moved to Florida, and my snow play was over. I realized that playing in the snow represented the time pre-explosion when my family's and my grandparents' homes were whole. Life was somewhat innocent; I didn't yet know about tragedy and pain.

My love of snow was not new but rather an old, forgotten relationship reborn. Seeing the heart-shaped snow wedged between the rocks was the beginning of my heart messengers. It told me I was right where I belonged, affirming that my path was best for me. Everything would be okay—and keep skiing!

It became common practice for me to look for hearts in my everyday doings. The Chinese believe that when someone is speaking and something gets broken, like a glass shattered onto the floor, it is a sign of truth. Hearts are my sign of truth.

Many people get inspiration from objects, like butterflies or crosses. It's a personal connection to something in the physical world that nudges you to trust that everything will be okay. I love when my friends see hearts and point them out to me or send me heart photos from afar, texting, "thinking of you." Of course, I also get eye rolls and smiles from my skeptical friends when I point out a heart-shaped object.

I sat with my dear friends Karen and Robert by the fire one evening, tossing around ideas of countries we longed to visit. Karen piped up, "Hey, Lesia, you should come to Vietnam with us! We're going next August with a few family members." Robert's father was married to Huong, a native of Vietnam. If I was going to Vietnam, I couldn't think of better travel companions than Karen and Robert with Huong leading the way.

I immediately reached for my phone to check the weather for August in Vietnam. Ask anyone with a burn injury— heat is tough to handle when your pores don't sweat to cool the body down. All desire to join my friends for this adventure was crushed when I read about the 95 percent humidity every day, all day.

I laid the phone down. "I'm out. It's going to be too hot." Karen's smile slumped, but she understood that hot weather left me deflated and irritated. I've always had a yearning to travel to a country rich in sacred temples, charming villages, and delicious food, frolicking in the history and culture. It was a hard decision not to go, yet in a spiritual way I felt as though I would still be there, somehow.

While on a layover on her way to Saigon, Karen called from the Los Angeles airport. "Lesia, I really wish you were with us. You have such good travel karma!"

"Karen, you know I would be miserable. The heat would turn me into a worthless travel companion. But you know I'm always with you guys. Just keep your eyes open and you will see me there. I can feel it!" They had been gone only a week when I received an email from Karen with the subject line, "I see you!"

They had visited Bai Dinh Pagoda, just outside of Hanoi. It is a large and ornate Buddhist temple, quite famous in the country, most memorable to Karen because of its three hundred steps. Many tourists stand at the first step and ponder if they can make the journey.

The group stood at the base of the ancient stone steps, not actually seeing the top, and discussed who, if anyone, was going to climb up to the top to experience the temple. Karen, Robert, their daughter (my goddaughter) Lauren, and Huong ventured up the ancient steps. Karen said she thought about me as she battled the heat. Once inside, it took a while to replenish their fluids, cool down, and catch their breath before they toured the temple and the magnificent primeval carvings.

When Karen and Lauren came upon one of many altars, they stood and marveled at the gilded sacred artifacts. Suddenly, a woman and her son stepped breathlessly into the temple and kneeled between Karen and Lauren and the altar. Karen wondered why they would squeeze themselves directly in front of them in this sacred space. Lauren saw it first. She gripped Karen's arm and tugged urgently, pointing to the back of the little boy's shirt. "Mom!" she whispered.

"It's Lesia. Look, she's here!" On the back of the little boy's powder blue T-shirt was a large sweat mark in the shape of a heart. When I received the photo, I knew I had made the right decision not to step into that hot, sweaty, yet beautiful country. A sweaty heart, I see you.

> *Open your eyes, daily. The questions are there to encourage you to look at all the things you cannot see. That's the place where the answers live.*

I've listened to my intuition mumbling to me for years. When I ignore the messages in my gut, the situation never turns out well. How many times have we said, "I knew it!" after the fact? Tuning in to our intuition is one thing; trusting and acting upon it takes courage and years to master. Hearts—the signs from my angels—help me marry the two.

Bruce and I bought a second home on a small lake in northern Florida. The property holds six massive live oak trees with moss swaying from the limbs. The trees are over three hundred years old, and they lend the surroundings a sense of safety and stability. The property oozes serenity: it's our place to exhale and escape the pace of California.

As much as the property felt like our safe haven, we had a neighbor whose energy always gnawed at my psyche. Something was a little off about him. I asked Bruce to build a six-foot fence between us. He balked. "C'mon, Lesia, he's a nice man. You're overthinking."

I knew I wasn't, and I convinced Bruce we had to do something to block the troubling energy. The next morning, Bruce shuffled off to Lowe's to buy fencing material. He came home with poles, shovels, cement, and thirty-five single wooden planks to appease my gut, in 90-degree heat. He worked all day. As the sun was setting, he called for me to look at his progress. I checked it out and gave praise on a job well done thus far.

That night, I lay in bed haunted by the expense and labor Bruce invested in the heat of the day to build this fence. I began to doubt myself. Maybe I should've given my theory on the neighbor's dark energy more time before I made it an issue. Was my gut overreacting?

I woke the next morning, poured a cup of hot coffee, and sauntered out to the fence. I couldn't believe my eyes: a heart shape in the grain of the wood formed by two separate planks nailed together. I ran to wake Bruce and drag him outside to show him my intuition was right. Confident in my decision, I immediately began to sleep better. The privacy is an added bonus. Within a month the heart faded due to extreme weather, but the serenity remains.

Recently, during a large remodel on our home, I made numerous trips to Home Depot to ruminate on the selection of tile. Afraid I would choose the wrong one, an expensive mistake, I would pick a few, come back home, and lay them on the ground to get a visual. Then I would go back for a few more. The process was time consuming. During one trip, I decided not to complicate matters—pick one tile and be done with it.

> *When too much time passes and I realize I haven't seen any heart-shaped objects, I know it's because my heart is closed.*

As I waited in line to pay, a construction worker stood in front of me. Right there, at my eye level, was a heart-shaped hole torn into his shirt. After asking the man's permission, I took a picture of it for my collection. When I got home, I saw that the tile was the perfect shade of blue to complement the patterned wallpaper. Sometimes, seeing hearts is just coincidence; other times, when I really need the help, I pay close attention.

We were leaving on a last-minute trip, and our regular groomer for Bently, my brilliant, chocolate-colored standard poodle, was booked solid. He really needed a bath. Plus, he behaves better for the dogsitter when he's freshly groomed. I searched around town for a groomer with immediate availability, a tall order. Reading reviews and making calls, I finally found a place. As I tugged Bently through their front door on appointment day, I looked up and saw a shadow of a heart on the ceiling. I knew we were right where we belonged. It was a small sign but one that reassured me that he would be okay here.

My sister Cindy, who traveled with me to Nova Scotia, came to visit and lay reading on the love seat in my courtyard. I peeked out and noticed she had fallen asleep. I felt gratitude that she was visiting and resting. She clearly needed some quiet time, but I was antsy because we usually hike or shop when she arrives. When she woke, she told me it was the best nap she had had in a long time and how relaxed she felt. I went into the courtyard to take her a drink and found a heart-shaped stain on the cushion at her feet. This heart told me I made the right decision to let her rest rather than hustle right out on a trail or to the shops.

I have noticed that when weeks go by and I don't see any heart-shaped objects, it's because my own heart is closed off to life's abundance. Maybe I'm stressed about something or consumed by worry. *Will the grant be accepted? What if my mother's health declines?* Hearts may be all around me, angels sending me messages, but I don't see them. It's a telltale sign I need to stop my negative thought cycle and trust the direction I'm headed.

Find your symbol; it's been looking for you.

Other times, hearts appear just because. No aha moments, meanings, agenda, or message. But there are always benefits to looking. By searching for hearts, I find myself discovering the beauty around me in the most mundane moment or object—a telltale sign that my heart is open to the world, to possibility, to meaning.

Sweaty heart in the temple in Vietnam

"Heart in Heaven" 117

Heart fence, Lake Helen, Florida

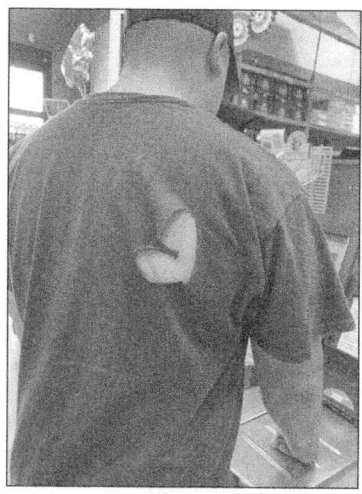

T-shirt heart, Home Depot customer    *Ceiling heart at the groomers*

Heart high above in the Sierras, California

Cushion heart in my courtyard, California

8
"I Got You"

We know more than we think we do.
It's extracting and conveying the knowledge
and its message to ourselves that is most difficult.
But sometimes that tiny voice inside
needs to stay quiet and let things be.

One morning in 2012, on my way to a meeting, my father called from Florida. His calls were entertaining; he often disguised his voice and pretended to be a cartoon character. Today, he just sounded motivated.

"Good morning, Baby, it's your father. What are you doing right now?"

"Good morning, Dad. I'm driving along the most beautiful stretch of the Pacific coast. What's up?"

"Baby, pull over. I need to talk to you."

"Are you okay, Dad? This sounds serious."

"Yes, I'm okay, but what I have to say needs your full attention."

He's up to something crafty. My thoughts flashed to a few years back when he called me every day asking if the pair of shoes he had bought me in Key West arrived. He insisted I needed to be home to sign for the shoes.

One evening, an enormous semi-trailer truck hauling several vehicles squeezed down our narrow lane and parked in front of our house. The driver, papers in his hand, walked up our steep driveway as Bruce opened the door. "Is Lesia home?" he asked. "I'm delivering a pair of shoes from her father."

He then offloaded a shiny new silver Lexus sedan with an enormous red bow attached to the hood and a tiny card that read, "Lesia." I called my father immediately. "Dad, love the shoes. They fit perfectly!"

"Gotcha!" he said and hung up.

I maneuvered my car onto a scenic overlook and parked. "Okay, Dad, I've pulled over now. What's up?" I glanced at the time, mindful of my upcoming meeting.

"Lesia, listen to me carefully. You need to call Warren Buffett and tell him about Angel Faces. He will fund your charity!" Could he tell I rolled my eyes? "Lesia, he's a smart man.

He'll detect your passion on the phone. Tell him how hard you've worked and about all the girls you've helped, and he will fund Angel Faces, I just know it! You must do this!"

"Dad, really? I have no access to Warren Buffet, and if I did, Warren Buffett does not know or care who I am or how hard I work or the girls I serve. Please, Dad, this is a crazy idea. How would I even get to him?"

"You've been on *Dr. Phil* and *CNN*. I'm sure Dr. Phil or Dr. Gupta knows his phone number and you know how to get in touch with them, right?" His enthusiasm was unrelenting.

Hearing without listening is meaningless. Stay silent to process what you hear, not to plan your response.

As I sat staring at the surf, listening to my father carry on about Warren Buffett and what he could do for me, I began to realize his clutch was slipping, cognitively. But I also realized how highly he thought of my capabilities. He wanted to encourage me to reach beyond what I had achieved. His vision of me and my accomplishments far exceeded my own. If only he had led by example, showing me what it took to be successful, not just dreaming up visions. I grew impatient with his grandiose plan, and now I was late for my meeting.

"Dad, I always appreciate your ideas. I'll investigate, I promise. I love you and I need to get to my meeting." I hung up and drove off.

A week passed and my father called again. I was hesitant to answer because I knew he would ask me about my call to Warren Buffett. The call I never made. We talked and laughed about everyday life, then said our goodbyes. Just before we hung up, he said, "Oh, wait! One more thing. How did your call go with Warren Buffett?"

"I haven't called yet, Dad, but I will." I lied.

Ten days later, my father died unexpectedly. I was at an annual conference on burns and trauma on the other side of the country when I got the shocking call at midnight from my sister. My grief could have stopped a freight train. However, buried in deep grief, I marched on. I still had to run Angel Faces.

When I started Angel Faces in 2003, I was laser focused on creating a safe place where girls, after their discharge from the hospital, could go to rest, learn skills, and find hope. Seeing the girls grow, find courage, and embrace their vulnerabilities became my fuel.

A decade later, I was growing tired of the operational management behind the scenes. There were budgets to create, meet, and maintain. Finding and keeping the right staff was essential. I also needed effective marketing, innovative program design, and well-trained volunteers. Most importantly, Angel Faces relied on donor cultivation and fundraising. I hated asking people for money. I never wanted to be the one people hid from when I walked into the room, afraid I would shake them down. I've always believed that when you do what you love, and do it well, the money will follow.

Angel Faces has been blessed with constant funding, but those blessings came from endless hard work. Not one development director I hired lasted more than nine months. It's the nature of nonprofits: high turnover due to low pay and minimal benefits. When I worked at a burn foundation prior to launching Angel Faces, I watched my employer raise lots of money. He kept adding more staff, bigger offices, and the latest computer equipment but not expanding programs. I didn't understand it and was embarrassed for him and determined not to lead with that business model. Angel Faces ran a lean operation and funneled everything we could toward the girls. I was proud that there was a short cord between our donations and the girls we served.

Knowing the emotional toll a retreat can take, I reminded my volunteers to rest and recharge beforehand. Yet, I was still going full throttle managing the day-to-day operations of the organization while also pushing for funding. I was not taking my own advice.

Days before the retreats, I arrived on site for training and prep already exhausted. The girls' arrival invigorated me, and I forgot that I needed rest. After the retreats, I came home with bloodshot eyes, tired feet, swollen fingers, and an achy back. In a hot bath, I closed my eyes and saw the past two weeks like a slideshow, watching the miracles and breakthroughs, like one of the girls wearing shorts or going without a wig for the first time since her injury. I've witnessed so many breakthroughs—courage in action. Some people go their whole lives and never witness one.

Over the years, every retreat took on its own energy, my involvement included. In New Hampshire, my medical and logistics team and I stayed at the private lake house three miles from the girls at Brewster. Midweek during a retreat in 2016, I woke early, immediately checking my phone for any reports from Brewster. All was quiet, so I had a few moments to myself.

I clicked over to my social media and found several posts of close friends hiking in Yosemite, swimming with dolphins in Mexico, biking in Utah, and riding in a gondola in Italy. Envy overcame my heart. *Why can't I be doing that?* I began to question my mission. I rose out of bed and looked at the stack of program materials to teach that day. To the right of the papers was my binder of all the girls' applications—trauma and pain written on every sheet. I didn't want to swim in their trauma anymore. I had my own from so many years ago. It was all too much.

> *When someone says, "Please pull over," know they have something important to say, if not for them but for you.*

As I brushed my teeth, I looked in the mirror and saw my scars. They stared back at me—still there. A constant reminder of that horrible experience decades ago. "When will they go away?" the girls often asked. By the time I showered and began to dress, my pity party was in full swing. I yearned to be frolicking in the outdoors like my friends, anywhere but here. *When will it be my turn to focus on what is good for me?*

I had no time to wallow. I had to practice what I preached, believe I belonged here, and, most importantly, bury this discontent from the girls and volunteers. This mindset would not sustain me for the full program ahead. I was here to hold the hearts of these wounded girls, to lead them toward hope as though they were my own daughters.

Later that morning, I led a session called "How to Handle Staring, Teasing, and Unwanted Questions." This is an important part of the week, as it addresses real-life situations the girls face on a daily basis. I looked at the circle of young, wounded faces, scarred and scared and hungry to learn how to cope. Suddenly, an epiphany of enormous gratitude came over me. I was right where I belonged, in this magnificent barn, deep in a sacred forest, with the girls, serving God. How dare I question my path and forget my angels' agreement?

Fighting tears of shame for pitying myself that morning, I told the girls to take a ten-minute break. As I turned for a tissue, Rosemary, whose face was severely disfigured, jumped up and propelled her little arms around my neck. "Do you even know how much you are helping me and all these girls? Ms. Lesia, you are changing our lives!" We cried together for different reasons. I allowed her words to wash away the morning's doubt. I did belong here today, tomorrow, and onward. No Yosemite hike, swimming with dolphins, or biking in Utah could've filled my heart and delivered the message I felt in this moment. It seems at my lowest times, something powerful happens.

Normal life felt surreal to me immediately after the intensity of the retreats. My family learned over time to stay clear for a few weeks so I could close up the wounds from the raw, painful stories I'd been exposed to. Bruce took me out to dinner, and I gazed around the room at the patrons and waiters, so beautiful and flawless, no scars, no missing body parts. They looked whole, like actors in a movie. My eyes fixated on their beauty as they laughed and dined, seemingly living an unblemished life. When the waiter came to take our order, I stared in awe at his perfect hands as he set down my glass of wine while smiling with his entire face intact.

"Are you ready to order?" the perfect smile asked.

After the retreats ended, I always hit the ground running to raise money for the next one. Usually, a miracle happened. A donor would step up with funding, and I'd be inspired to continue. It seemed like Groundhog Day. The best days post-retreat were when I received powerful messages from the girls about how they conquered a life challenge because of what they learned at Angel Faces.

Adriana called me after one retreat. "Lesia! I'm at Cedar Point! The amusement park! At Cedar Point! Can you believe it?"

"Well, good! I'm glad you are enjoying yourself."

"No, Lesia! I am at *Cedar Point . . . with my family!*" She went on to explain that she could never go to the amusement park with her family because all the people would stare at her badly scarred face. She would end up crying and the family would take turns sitting in the car with her. The family then decided it was best she stay home every year with her grandmother to avoid repeating the bad experience. I flashed back to shopping with my grandparents and the angst that always ensued for all of us. I thought about the public events I refrained from if I wasn't feeling strong enough to field the stares.

At the retreat, Adriana learned how to begin to love herself, embrace her looks, and handle people when they stared or asked unwanted questions by responding with grace and kindness. "Lesia, I'm standing in line at the entrance. People are staring at me, and I'm smiling and waving hello back to them and they are smiling back at me! This is the best day ever!"

Adriana felt like I was there at the amusement park rejoicing with her. Teaching the girls strength through my pain was worth it. Stories like Adriana's kept me going, but I was slowly running out of stamina to endure the grueling demands of fundraising between each retreat.

After New Hampshire in 2016, I'd had to fire my program director on the last day of the retreat. She had flown home ahead of me, cleaned out her desk, pitched her files, and emptied the petty cash. I had forgotten to tell my landlord to change the locks. I walked into Angel Faces' empty office with a mountain of wrap-up paperwork that would take weeks to complete. I set my things down on my desk, including my head, and silently wept.

I wanted to be done. But before I could close my door for good, I had to write a massive number of thank-you letters, organize receipts, finalize budgets, write reports, unpack boxes, and inventory supplies arriving from New Hampshire. The post-retreat checklist seemed endless, especially without a program director.

> *Knowing we are right where we belong can bring us peace. Yet, it also gives us a clear starting point; which direction we turn is up to us. The scarecrow is of no help. Trust yourself.*

The requisite fundraising events where guests arrived in tight garments and toe-pinching shoes especially taxed me and my limited team. They required months of planning, budgeting, the involvement of volunteers who were already worn out from the retreat, and the writing of more thank-yous. If you are going to do something, best to go all out on the details, but that comes with a price of time, talent, and treasure.

I told God that if He wanted me to continue this work, I needed people who believed in Angel Faces' mission and would support us without the three-ring circus of a fundraising gala. I needed a miracle.

I was just getting to the backside of my post-retreat to-do list when a cherished volunteer sent me through snail mail a clipping from the *Boston Globe* announcing that Doris

Buffett (Warren's sister) was "giving all her money away" to those in great need. The article went on to say that Doris's goal was to make her last check bounce. My volunteer attached a little note that read, "Lesia, maybe you should write to Doris and ask if she will support Angel Faces."

Thinking of my prayer for major donors to lift my burden, I wrote Doris a brief letter and included my first book, *Heart of Fire*. Not long after, I received a generic email stating Angel Faces did not qualify for funding from Doris's foundation. I was deflated but still slightly hopeful. *I didn't get this far to only get this far.*

I was on to the next grant application when I received an email from a source I didn't recognize—someplace called the Letters Foundation. The email said, "At this time, the Foundation is not processing requests from organizations. However, upon further review of your work, we would love to learn more about the impact you have on the people you serve." They requested many documents, including annual reports, budgets, testimonials, profit and loss statements, and a proposal. Despite the vague message, my gut told me to trust the source. I sent the documents, blocking out banking information and account numbers.

The next two Mondays, I received requests for additional documents with a deadline of Friday. They also requested that all the information be condensed to one page. The demands were becoming preposterous for a small nonprofit like Angel Faces with a full-time staff of one. On a phone call, a contact from the foundation asked for a three-to-five-year proposal. I asked for guidelines, and she put it back on me. "Ask for whatever you'd like!" This was a nightmare game of ping-pong. I alerted my graphic artist, summoned my board treasurer, and laser focused the document to one page. I kept believing that you just never know what a connection can bring. I had to stay open and eternally hopeful, despite my insecurities.

Finally, the woman I had been communicating with explained that the Letters Foundation was led by Doris Buffett. A few weeks later, I contacted Doris's team to tell them I was coming to Boston for a speaking engagement and asked if we could meet in person. They agreed but made it very clear that our meeting was slated for just thirty minutes.

I arrived in Boston during a snowstorm and checked into my hotel. I had a sleepless night caught between jet lag and excitement about my upcoming meeting and presentation. With puffy eyes from forced heat, I grabbed a coffee and jumped into an Uber headed for the vicinity of the address, which I was asked not to share with anyone.

Shuffling down an icy, quaint street of brownstones, boutiques, and cafés, all covered in fresh snow, I knew I was being watched by my angels. The setting was picture perfect.

I stopped at a massive cement heart on display in a lovely women's boutique. I knew it was a sign. I made a mental note to return for some retail therapy after the meeting. I might need to self-soothe with a new sweater.

As I turned from the heart, my eyes locked on a concealed keypad next to a plain door. The numbers above the door matched my instructions. I was here. I drew a breath and punched in the code. The three women I met were as real as rain. We sat around a table and discussed Angel Faces and life in general, tripling our allotted time together. We said our goodbyes with a promise to be in touch. I stopped at the boutique with the cement heart in the window, but there was nothing that appealed to me. My own heart was already full, no hole to fill with fabrics or baubles.

Days after I arrived back in San Diego, I received a FedEx package with a large check. Doris Buffett had funded a retreat. This was God winking back at me. No fundraiser to run, just a check to renew my hope. I felt energized!

During the retreat, I received word that a few ladies from Doris's foundation were coming to the VIP night. We are a closed retreat, meaning we don't allow people to come and go throughout the week. This creates a safe environment for the girls. On VIP night, we invite a small handful of major donors to see our work firsthand. That night, a few ladies shuffled in who carried the softness of anyone's grandmother, tender hearted and oozing compassion without being overly sentimental. Their humility was an energy I admire in my donors. No fanfare, no waving flags, just purely generous women wanting to see where the donations were going.

Back home after the retreat, I received a call from two of the women I met on that snowy day in Boston. They were thrilled to share that Doris's foundation had granted Angel Faces funds for the next three years of retreats. I was certain my tears would short out the electronics in my iPhone. It took me weeks to touch the ground again.

God listens to us. However, He does get the last word.

It had been over four years since my father passed. On my way to the bank with the first installment, I could hear him laughing. "See, Baby, I told you to call Warren Buffett."

"Okay, Dad, you win. But it wasn't Warren, it was his sister," I whispered back.

My father nudged me from heaven. "Same family, Baby, same family."

Having someone believe in us is sometimes all we need in our life. My father believed I could do anything and told me so often. Doris Buffett, in the form of her grant to Angel Faces, arrived in my life when I needed it most. She said, "I got you. I'm here to help," but it came through in the voice of my dad, my angel.

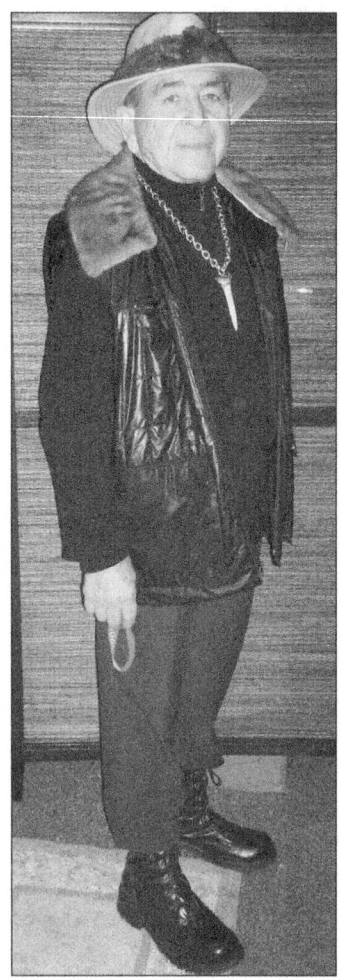

My father

9
Tumbleweed

*We can attempt to run from inevitable circumstances,
but adjusting our speed sometimes isn't enough
to avoid the collision. If we get caught,
it's crucial not to panic; simply slow down and
allow a few strangers to pull away the debris.*

My work demands all my emotional reserves. To balance the heavy lifting of emotions, I self-soothe with outdoor adventures mixed with a little risk. I prefer the kind of activity where your hair is blown out, sun and wind have sizzled your face, and your body tingles with exhaustion.

I surprised Bruce on his birthday with a new Harley-Davidson Road King Classic, 100th Anniversary Edition motorcycle. After riding with him as his passenger for a year, he bought me my own bike: a new shiny, black-and-white Softail Deluxe Harley loaded with chrome.

Bruce was quick to critique my riding skills. I had passed all the riding classes, but this was a large bike for me at

825 pounds with a 1450cc engine. He knew I was careful and extremely aware, but that didn't stop him from tossing advice my way. "Lesia, you go too slow. You are an impediment to traffic—you need to speed up!" I bantered back that I would ride in my comfort zone until I was ready to advance.

"Lesia, don't wrestle with your bike; trust your skill level and simply ride it. Take command of the road and the direction you're headed."

Then the opportunity presented itself. I decided to cruise the coast on a beautiful sunny afternoon. As I approached a small hill, I laid on the throttle, trying to get out of a blind spot in the neighboring lane. A motor officer with the Carlsbad Police Department suddenly appeared in the lanes with his hand up, blowing his whistle for all lanes of traffic to stop. My eyes gleamed at his shiny knee-high black leather boots. I wanted a pair, badly. That was going to be my next purchase. I made a move to ride around him. He blew his whistle louder and moved in front of me. "You!" He pointed at me. "Pullover—now!"

I pointed to my own chest and mouthed, "Who, me?"

He sternly pointed his gloved finger from me to the curb in an exaggerated gesture. I was in trouble. I didn't know whether to feel like a badass or duly embarrassed. He continued to hold up all the traffic while I downshifted to first gear and crossed over in front of all the cars to reach the curb with my feet walking my bike the rest of the distance. As he approached, he wasted no time. "I need to see your license, registration, and insurance."

When I'm on my bike, I take my time, focus, and go through the steps with my gear. I can't let anything rush, rattle, or rock me. One missed step like forgetting to click your helmet or not securing your purse strap can cost you your life.

I began my process of shutting down my bike, checking I was not in gear or parking in sand. I eased the 825 pounds onto its kickstand, turned off my music, removed my gloves and stuffed them where they wouldn't fall off, released my helmet latch, and balanced it on the handlebars, fixed my helmet hair, and then stood to throw a leg over. Finally, I unlatched my saddlebag to retrieve the requested documents. I could see the officer was frustrated but amused at my tenacity. I was well trained, and it showed.

"Do you know why I stopped you?" he asked. I noticed a police cruiser parked a little distance ahead of his motorcycle with an officer pointing a radar gun at the traffic coming up the hill.

"No, I don't," I lied. "Was I going too slow? Are my pipes too loud?"

"You are too loud. Do you know what the speed limit is on this stretch of road?" I shook my head no. "The speed limit here is 35 miles per hour. I clocked you at 53!" He showed me the 53 MPH on his radar screen.

"Oh, Officer, I think you are dyslexic!" I smiled.

He tried to conceal his smile. "You were speeding."

I handed him my license, registration, and insurance. Trying to charm him in chatty conversation, I told him my husband thought I rode too slowly and was an impediment to traffic. He seemed to like my use of the word "impediment."

The officer took my documents and swaggered over to his partner in the patrol car. Watching their body language as they leaned on the hood of their squad car, I saw they were laughing. I had to think quickly. I didn't want a speeding ticket, but I wanted proof in writing that I was speeding so I could show my husband. I flipped the approach.

As he sauntered back, I noticed his edge dissolving. "Officer, are you going to give me a ticket? I really don't want a ticket. I have a clean driving record. But I want to show my husband some sort of proof that I am not an impediment to traffic like he insists I am and that I was speeding! And Officer, could you please call my husband on his cell phone right now and tell him you've got me on the side of the road, caught me speeding on my Harley? And be sure to tell him how fast I was going!"

The officer declined to call my husband, but he opened up his citation pad and began writing. "Here, put this on your refrigerator. Make sure your husband sees it tonight." I thanked him and we said our goodbyes.

I got my gear and I pulled away slowly, gently laying on the throttle. He forgot to ticket me on my illegal loud pipes, and I wasn't up for a police chase. It makes my heart squeeze when blessings come from angst. As soon as I returned home, the warning citation went up on the refrigerator for Bruce to inspect.

Now that I was officially qualified to keep up with him on the Harley, with the warning notice to prove it, we decided to take a three-week road trip to the Canadian border from our home in Southern California. We packed our bikes with the bare necessities: rain gear, extra helmet, boots, leather chaps, safety glasses, tools, and toiletries, in addition to a few items of clothing. It's amazing how little you need on a daily basis. We perused maps and made a list of places we wanted to see. Our intention was to ride back roads, not freeways, and no set schedule.

With cash in our pocket and our dog sitter, Michelle, prepared to care for our standard poodles, Fargo and Cynder (Bently had not been born yet, or he would've never let me go away that long), we rolled out of our driveway with adventure in our hearts, an open road ahead, and only a return date.

I added one more step to my usual pre-ride checklist. The moment just prior to our nod that we were ready to roll, I placed my hands together to pray for protection, smooth riding, seamless operative mechanics, and abundant beauty. Sometimes my prayers went a little too long for Bruce, but he needed to hear them.

The common question people asked us about the trip was what type of radio communication we used between our helmets. None. We came up with a set of hand signals: potty breaks, fuel, food, and the big one, acknowledging the beauty around us. That was all we needed. Focusing on an open road with a powerful machine between your legs can keep you very busy.

Early into the trip, we were riding on a two-lane back road outside of New Meadows, Idaho. The late afternoon sun cast a golden hue across the acres of crops. We needed to find dinner and a place to stay for the night. The town was three blocks long, and everything was shut down. Storefronts looked like they'd been closed for decades. As we rolled out of town, we passed a home with a banner flapping over the door that read, "Fire Department BBQ Tonight 6–8 p.m." We both saw it at the same time. No hand signals needed, we slowed down and pulled into the small gravel lot next to a few cars.

The backyard was filled with firefighters, farmers, and their families dishing out heaps of creamed corn casseroles, potato salads, coleslaw, and the main show, the barbecue meat. Cherry and apple pies were displayed on separate tables. As we cleared the door, a hush came over the yard. All eyes fell on us. We were getting used to the hush when we entered rooms or restaurants dressed in leathers with windblown hair like some Hells Angels who have arrived to shoot up the place. But with Bruce wearing a baseball cap with San Diego Fire across the top, I was expecting a warmer welcome.

We stood in the short ticket line at a rickety cardboard table to pay our five dollars for a meal. With our plates full, we squeezed into one side of a picnic table and exchanged polite niceties with the folks three planks away, yet we still felt like strangers among this fire family. We ate in silence.

Bruce took a bite of his barbecue sandwich and immediately put his hand to his mouth. A cap on this front tooth, which had been placed forty-five years ago, broke off, leaving him with a huge gap. He now whistled when he spoke. The folks across from us began to laugh. The old farmer at the edge of the table looked up and said, "Well, looky here. Now I'll betcha you feel right at home with us." The ice was broken, and we were now part of their fire family. After we finished our meal and warm conversations, they followed us out with pies wrapped in tinfoil. Vulnerability bonds us.

We rode another two thousand miles on back roads through the most beautiful landscape this country has to offer. We stopped at farmers markets and random antique shops and stayed in cute boutique hotels, often by rushing rivers. Hotels with laundry facilities and Jacuzzis took precedence. When I found unique items like embroidered linens made by cloistered nuns in Nebraska, I made multiple trips to the post office to ship treasures home. Bruce told me I couldn't carry another ounce on my bike.

Glacier National Park was massive and green, yet I was haunted by the fear of being chased by a grizzly bear. I would've preferred to be hiking on nature trails, not on a loud motorcycle, when experiencing the park. But with my "Embrace the choice" mantra, I was content. Yellowstone was equally magnificent, especially when an enormous bison sauntered onto the road in front of Bruce's bike, clearly signaling who had the right-of-way. We shut the bikes off and remained still, respecting and watching the beast for what seemed a long and nervous time.

We had been on the road fifteen days. I was growing tired, and it showed. I was windburned, sunburned, dehydrated, and endured never-ending numb buttocks. I was also getting irritated at continuously having to pick bugs out of my teeth, an act I was once proud of. At least I didn't have the bigger bugs that were getting stuck in the gap of Bruce's missing cap. *Who cares about a little gnat between mine?* I tried to tell myself.

We planned to leave Wyoming at 4:00 a.m. to beat the notorious winds and scorching temperatures. Bruce was always willing to ride before dawn to protect my scarred skin from the sweltering heat. I loved riding with him. He's a good road warrior, and not having helmet-to-helmet communication was a blessing. Can you imagine that whistle coming over the sound waves into my helmet?

After 120 miles on dark, windy back roads, the sun came up. We rolled into a mom-and-pop restaurant for breakfast. As we entered the first set of doors, Bruce made a hard right into the men's room. "I'll grab a table; see you inside," I mumbled over my shoulder. I pushed through a second set of doors and was met with the familiar hush by the other customers.

I found myself starting to shrink. *What is a little girl like me doing riding a huge Harley-Davidson motorcycle on a big, long road trip? I miss my dogs, my bed, and the comforts of home*. The longing for home had started to build a few days ago, but I never told Bruce. We had another 335 miles to go that day to make it to my friend's house in Reno by sunset.

By the time we got to a truck stop outside Salt Lake City, I was melting down. After sticking to back roads for weeks, now we were forced to ride on Interstate 80. At a busy truck stop, about fifteen semi-trailer trucks were fueling or parked with diesel engines running. Campers, RVs, cars, and people were everywhere. The fumes gagged me, and it was hot.

We pulled up at the store first because Bruce had to pee, again. I got off my bike next to him and went inside to cool off. He came out of the restroom, took one look at me, and sensed my weariness. "Lesia, let's go over here in the food area, cool down, and get something to eat."

We sat in a dirty plastic orange booth. While I picked the bugs out of my teeth, I looked up at the menu of fried food and sugary drinks. I wished for a green salad and some iced tea. "Bruce, I want to call Michelle and see how our babies are doing. I really miss them."

"Geez, Lesia, they are fine!" He got up to order.

Bruce returned with two hot dogs and drinks as I cried on the phone with Michelle. I tilted the phone away. "Michelle told me that she can sense Fargo and Cynder really miss us and asked when we were coming home." I handed the phone to Bruce, let my head fall on the sticky table, and sobbed.

Bruce chatted with Michelle, then hung up and took a bite of his hot dog. "Are you really crying? There is no crying at a truck stop, especially when you're wearing leathers and riding your Harley. We are just days from home!"

"I don't care. I'm done; I'm tired. It's been too many days where I've had to be physically strong, aware, upright, navigating danger that looms at every mile. I want to go home." I continued to sob. People began to notice.

Bruce lowered his voice. "Lesia, we are Reno-bound. Your friends are expecting us—we have no other option. We have three days left to get home. Eat your hot dog, drink your Coke, and go to the bathroom. We're going to fuel up at the pumps and take the highway straight to Reno. Stop crying. This is not the time or place for tears!" He got up and clomped to his bike.

I threw a leg over my bike and rolled behind him to the gas pumps. With my helmet clicked in and safety riding sunglasses securely in place, no one could tell I was weeping. As soon as I got on the highway, I could cry all I wanted, as loud as I needed, and no one could tell me to stop. My five-year-old self was fully present.

As Bruce fueled up our bikes, I looked over and saw a truck driver with his belly falling below his T-shirt nearly to his thighs. He was missing teeth and unshaven, with a few greasy hairs lying sparingly on his head. I could feel his eyes undressing me. As soon as he got my attention, he made a vulgar gesture with his mouth. I wanted to puke. Bruce was already upset with me for my shrinking energy, so I wouldn't get his sympathy. I quickly capped my gas tank and shouted, "Let's go; we're out of here!" I jumped on my bike, throttled up, and we pulled onto the highway headed straight for Reno.

I was angry over how tired I had allowed myself to become; I should have asked for a break sooner. A few days off at a spa would have helped. I seemed to have lost my voice, keeping things bottled up until I reached a breaking point. I wished Bruce had said, "Let's find a great luxury hotel and stay for a few days so you can rest and reset." But I had taught him that I was tough and could conquer nearly anything—and he believed me. I felt powerless, upset, and vulnerable that I had to ride this Harley for three more days. This is not a good mindset while you are on a bike.

My anger continued to bloom. I throttled up to ninety miles per hour and passed him. I wanted to get away from all the challenges of the day, including Bruce. Flying by him at ninety miles per hour made it clear he could never say I ride too slowly again. He watched me go by and shook his head while maintaining his legal speed. There was open land as far as you could see on both sides of the empty highway. Out of my right eye, I spied a large tumbleweed far away that was rapidly rolling toward me. I began to adjust my speed to avoid it. Remember in math class when a vehicle is traveling at a rate of speed x and another vehicle is traveling in the opposite direction at a rate of y? I wished I had paid attention in that class.

The variables I couldn't control were the tumbleweed and the wind. The only thing I could control was my speed, which I kept adjusting to avoid a collision. I had to stop crying and pay attention. When I slowed down, seemingly so did the tumbleweed. When I sped up, there she was picking up speed again. In riding school, you learn to never get singularly focused. You must always be scanning for potentially dangerous events and never swerve for an animal. That's when you can lose control. I also learned that freeways are the safest to ride as your chances of getting T-boned by a car coming from a perpendicular direction are null. Nothing was mentioned about a tumbleweed.

Despite my calculations, I hit that tumbleweed dead on. It was now wrapped around my hot engine, pieces of dry twigs shooting into my mouth and nose. I was most terrified that the remnants wedged in my hot engine would catch fire. With alternating hands, one reaching down and the other on the handlebars, I pulled debris off my bike while trying to maintain control and searching for the next exit. I needed to pull over.

The 4:00 a.m. launch from Wyoming, the exhaustion, sweltering heat, longing for home, my dogs, the trucker's sick gesture, and now this giant tumbleweed. I must've looked like Pigpen, riding in a dust ball. All I could think was that I somehow had to keep calm and control the 825 pounds of metal and gasoline carrying me down the highway and find the next exit. Motorcycles know no forgiveness. At the slightest flinching, you can easily lose control. My conversation with San Diego Police Department's only female motor officer, Laurie Bach, flashed through my head. "Lesia, don't wrestle with your bike, ride it. You own it and the road!" I felt my strength flooding back. *You got this. Dry your damn tears and woman up!*

Channeling Peter Fonda in Easy Rider was thrilling, until the tumbleweed appeared.

One of our many agreements at the beginning of this trip was that if we had a problem or got separated on the road, we would get off at the next exit and wait to hear from each other. Knowing Bruce was behind me and had probably witnessed my collision with the tumbleweed, I figured he would surely follow me off at the next exit. He didn't. As I looked up from the ramp, he cruised by on the overpass. I rode into the first shelter I could find, popped off my bike, and began pulling the rest of the tumbleweed away from the scorching engine.

It's easy to get help when you're a girl on a Harley. A few guys rushed over and helped me remove the dirty debris from my engine while I pulled twigs off my chaps. It wasn't long before Bruce showed up. "Well, baby, that was quite a show," he shouted through his helmet. "That was the biggest tumbleweed I've ever seen!" He laughed. Apparently, he had witnessed the whole thing but wanted to give me a few minutes to sort myself out.

I thought about that tumbleweed on the rest of the ride to Reno. Originally imported from Russia, tumbleweed is a hardy bush that breaks free of the root when it dries out and travels by wind, spreading seeds. As it rolls, it picks up sticks and debris. It's like human pain in many ways. An old wound picks up debris—bias, doubt, negativity—as it travels toward us, growing and festering when not addressed. As much as we try to avoid it as I did by speeding up and slowing down, it is sometimes destined to hit us. Maybe it's to teach us a valuable lesson, or to get us to stop and remove what is toxic or what can hurt us in our lives.

The longer a tumbleweed rolls, the bigger it gets, and the longer it travels, the more seeds it spreads. Like the effects of a traumatic event when untreated by a professional, not talked about and stuffed deep into our being, it expands and spreads the seeds of hurt, shame, and fear. It will eventually force us off our path. My accident in my grandparents' house was the tumbleweed that slammed into my grandfather, rendering him almost delirious with pain that afternoon in the ambulance.

I could've pulled over when I first noticed the tumbleweed in my peripheral vision barreling across the landscape. But I tried to maneuver around it, thinking I could beat it. I've done this in life, too. Rather than take the easy way—avoidance—I've often chosen to blaze a path, knowing full well it may put me on a collision course with my trauma. In many ways—like Angel Faces—it has paid off. In other ways, not so much. When confronting my pain has gone terribly wrong, it was because I wasn't ready. I hadn't done the healing work I needed to do.

When I was twenty-one, a friend invited me to be part of her ground crew at a hot air balloon race. My duty was simply to hold tight to one of the many ropes that tethered the basket to the ground while the flame's heat filled the balloon. The competitors soon hopped into the basket and waited for one more teammate before the launch whistle blew. Time ticked away with no teammate in sight. Finally, my friend signaled for me to come and jump into the basket for the balloon race.

Remember my adventurous spirit, my self-soothing with windblown hair and bugs in my teeth? I jumped into the basket, the whistle blew, and we launched into the air with nine other balloons. It was thrilling for a moment until I realized I was trapped in mid-air with hundreds of gallons of propane and a twenty-eight-foot flame above my head. Running from this danger was not an option. Terrified beyond words, I teetered on the edge of a panic attack. The balloon race lasted longer than seemed possible. When we landed on a golf course, I was the first one out of the basket. I ran from the balloon, dropped to my knees, and wept.

I realized that day that my traumatic experience of being burned still lived in my body, even twelve years after the explosion. I had frozen in fear as though my accident was yesterday. I operated in a state of "I'm fine" to teach my family and the world to treat me normally, but my reaction to the balloon ride was not normal. I began to recognize how present my trauma still was: I wouldn't live in an apartment fueled by natural gas, and I dreaded filling up the gas tank in my car. Rather than seek professional counseling, I layered on coping skills, mostly avoidance, to minimize my fears.

Trauma, untreated, will chase you down. I finally stopped running. I went to therapy, and I went into a burning building with Bruce's guidance and protection. That's when my healing truly began. Since then, I've healed on so many levels that I can live a full life. I understand that treasure can be found in trauma. I wish my grandfather and the countless others of his generation had been able to heal their wounds rather than build a life dedicated to avoiding them.

I cried all the way to Reno. Bill and Rae, my friends for the past thirty years, heard the roar of our bikes and met us in their driveway. I shut off the bike and removed my helmet. Rae shrieked, "Lesia, you look like hell!" Even with this welcome, Rae was a soft place to land on a very hard day. We ate a fabulous meal, sipped cold martinis, and enjoyed a lot of laughs. As hard as the previous day of riding was, I found myself excited for the next. We departed early in the morning for home.

We all have our tumbleweeds that we try to avoid. Big balls of trauma that have picked up toxic thoughts, failures, low self-worth, unresolved issues, and disappointments. They roll toward us, sometimes fast, sometimes slow, becoming larger the longer we ignore them. Despite our actions to avoid them, they can overtake us. After impact, we pick off the debris so it doesn't create a bigger problem like a fire. And out of nowhere, strangers appear to help, dusting us off, reassuring, and helping us to prepare for what lies ahead.

Tumbleweed 153

Me on the road to Reno, Nevada.

Final Thoughts

Since I have finished this book, more of life unfolds.

My relationship with Brewster in Wolfeboro, New Hampshire, strengthens. I continue to have deep gratitude for the family who so generously donates their slice of private heaven for Angel Faces and the girls we serve. The family's property and Brewster have been part of Angel Faces' cradle of retreats for the past ten years. The private property offers something special for our girls who come so wounded and leave elated and hopeful for their future. We are grateful for the collaboration. We also have retreats in San Diego and Tennessee when budgets allow.

Lux called me recently and told me she is applying for a position with a large research company. Her interview was fast approaching, and she didn't know if she should pin her hair back for the interview. Would they be horrified at the scars on her face? she asked. She didn't know what to do. I could feel her anxiety across the miles. After a few deep conversations about self-love and owning our truth, Lux pinned her hair up, revealing her face. She went through three more interviews and landed the position with the company of her dreams. When we accept how we look, so will others.

It's been several years since Bruce never gave up on Katie in the gangway. Each time I board a plane, I pause in the gangway to remind myself of that magical evening when wings sprouted from the backs of those around me. As I drag my luggage to the plane, time is too tight to tell the story to my fellow passengers in the boarding queue. I reflect on the fragility of life, with gratitude for the lesson Katie left with us.

Sam left Parkland, Florida, for New York to distance herself from haunting reminders of that horrible day. She is working on a film about shootings and PTSD, which takes her to many high schools. She found that advocacy work and pouring her pain into art and film design help her to heal. "It's been a bumpy road. Some days are worse than others, but transforming my pain makes me feel braver and more whole." When I asked her if she found the gift in the trauma yet, she shared that at whatever facility she enters, she immediately looks for the exits and knows she has what it takes to help people out of the building should the need to evacuate arise.

Sadly, Doris Buffett died a few years ago. I never had the honor of meeting her personally, but I feel her continuous love and support with every retreat. After her passing, I received a call telling me that her foundation would continue to support Angel Faces, one of just a few charities that were chosen. I'm deeply humbled by her continuous generosity. May she rest peacefully.

I continue my laser treatments with Dr. Vic Ross, director at Scripps Clinic Laser and Cosmetic Dermatology Center in San Diego. He and Dr. Waibel are legends in their field, and I'm beyond blessed to be in their care. Although I still wrestle with the pain demons of the past, medications help to endure while I visualize the laser burning away the self-judgments we place on ourselves.

I plan on visiting my family in Halifax, Nova Scotia, again. This time I'm determined to see only the beauty, appreciate the healing the city has embraced, hear some whaling stories, visit old pubs, and focus on the picturesque harbor side city it has become.

I still ride my Harley, but most days I prefer my Vespa, trading leathers for a long skirt and boots for sneakers. Besides, they are more agile to chase down tumbleweeds.

—Lesia

Lesia Stockall Cartelli

Founder, chief executive officer of Angel Faces, a motivational speaker, and author of *Heart of Fire*. She carries her audience and readers on a path of her adventures of laughter to tears and back again.

She lives in Southern California with her husband Bruce and Bently, her beloved chocolate standard poodle.

Bring Lesia Cartelli to your next event.

LesiaSC@LesiaCartelli.com

LesiaCartelli.com

Angel Faces, established in 2003, is a 501c3 national nonprofit that provides intensive educational and healing regional retreats and ongoing support for girls and young women with burn/trauma injuries. The mission is to inspire and empower them to reach their optimum potential and develop meaningful relationships with themselves, their families, and their communities. If you'd like to make a donation, become a corporate partner or attend a retreat, visit *AngelFaces.com*.

angel faces

CELEBRATING 20 YEARS • HEADS UP, WINGS OUT

Heart of Fire
An Intimate Journey of Pain, Love, and Healing

Lesia Stockall Cartelli

"Lesia Cartelli is a courageous soul who has met and learned from the incredible hardship life has given her. Our reward is her enormous heart and commitment to guide us through."
— MARK NEPO, *New York Times* best-selling author of *The Book of Awakening*

What happens when a young girl playing hide-and-seek with her cousin in her special hiding place suddenly turns into an exploding inferno? Nine-year-old Lesia Cartelli lived through the total demolition of her grandparents' home that resulted in burns covering 50 percent of her body and face.

You will discover her scars are her gift as you learn that Lesia attracts people to her heart. She is the founder and guiding light of Angel Faces a national nonprofit life-changing organization that creates retreats and ongoing support for adolescents and young women who have severe burn/trauma injuries. Her personal goal is for us to embrace trauma, not allow it to define us.

Carlyle Press | 978-0-9904307-3-5 | $19.95

Made in the USA
Middletown, DE
27 May 2024